Samuel Orchart] [Beeton, George Rose Emerson

Jon Duan, a Twofold Journey With Manifold Purposes

Samuel Orchart] [Beeton, George Rose Emerson

Jon Duan, a Twofold Journey With Manifold Purposes

ISBN/EAN: 9783744799904

Printed in Europe, USA, Canada, Australia, Japan

Cover: Foto ©Andreas Hilbeck / pixelio.de

More available books at **www.hansebooks.com**

A Twofold Journey

With Manifold Purposes.

BY THE AUTHORS OF

"THE COMING K——" and "THE SILIAD."

Contents:

DEDICATION . .	. *Ben Trovato.*
CANTO THE FIRST .	. *Ancestry, Parentage, and Education.*
CANTO THE SECOND .	*The Queenless Court.*
CANTO THE THIRD .	*Progress through Bohemia.*
CANTO THE FOURTH .	. *Mother Church and her Children.*
CANTO THE FIFTH .	. *The Savour of Society.*
CANTO THE SIXTH .	*The Lords and Ladies of the Drama.*
CANTO THE SEVENTH	. *A Sojourn in Deer Land.*
CANTO THE EIGHTH	*The Smoke-Room at the M—— Club.*

London:
WELDON & CO., 15, WINE OFFICE COURT, FLEET STREET, E.C.
1874.

JON DUAN ADVERTISEMENTS.

E. MOSES & SON,
Merchant Tailors and Outfitters for all Classes.

OVERCOATS in Great Variety, 19s. to £7.
The Newest Styles and Patterns.

Extensive Preparations have been made in every Department for the Winter Season.

A DISTINCT DEPARTMENT FOR BOYS' CLOTHING.

ALL GOODS MARKED IN PLAIN FIGURES.	RULES FOR SELF-MEASURE.
Any article Exchanged, or, if desired, the money returned.	Patterns, List of Prices, and Fashion Sheet, Post Free.

E. MOSES & SON'S Establishments are Closed every Friday evening at sunset till Saturday evening at sunset, when business is resumed till eleven o'clock.

The following are the only Addresses of E. MOSES & SON:

LONDON
- CORNER OF MINORIES AND ALDGATE.
- NEW OXFORD STREET, CORNER OF HART STREET.
- CORNER OF TOTTENHAM COURT ROAD & EUSTON ROAD.

COUNTRY BRANCH—BRADFORD, YORKSHIRE.

MUSICAL BOX DEPOTS, 56, Cheapside; and 22, Ludgate Hill.

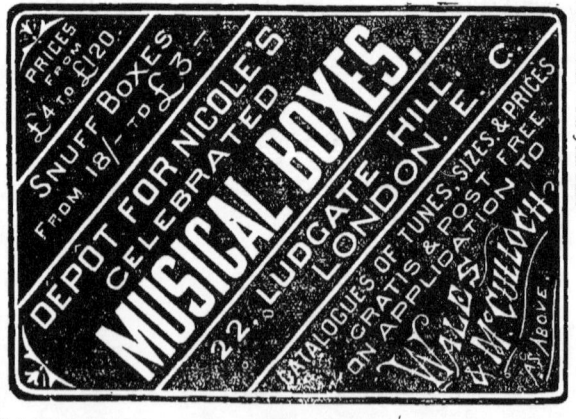

WATCHES AT ABOUT HALF-PRICE,

By eminent makers (FRODSHAM, M'CABE, BARRAUD, DENT, &c.), in Gold and Silver, quite unimpaired by wear; the system of warranty ensuring complete satisfaction to purchasers. Catalogues, with prices, gratis and post free on application.

WALES & M'CULLOCH, 22, Ludgate Hill; and 56, Cheapside, London.

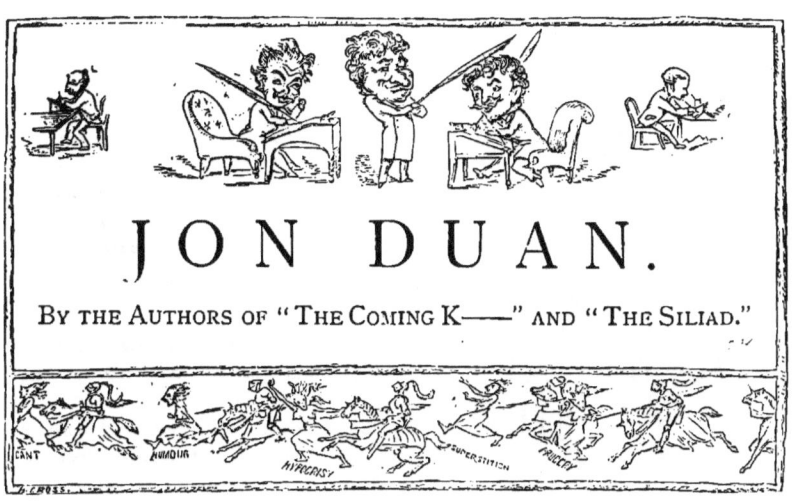

JON DUAN.

BY THE AUTHORS OF "THE COMING K——" AND "THE SILIAD."

Dedication.

BEN DIZZY! you're a humbug—Humbug-
    laureate,
And representative of all the race;
Although 'tis true that you turned out a Tory at
    Last, yours is still an enigmatic face.
And now, O Sphyntic renegade, what are you at
    With all the Rurals in and out of place?
Where will you leave the boobies in the lurch—
Have you resolved to double D—— the Church?

You've dished the Whigs before; we now would
    sing,
What is the pie that you're so busy making?
A dainty dish to set before the Thing—
    Or aught that its digestion will be shaking?—
Or is it Discord's apple that you bring?
    Or will you set the good old Tories quaking,
By saying that they hitherto have missed tricks,
By not going in for equal polling districts?

You'll educate them, won't you, Master Ben?
    And make them think that they are clever,
        very,
Until the trick is won, and they'll wish, then,
    They'd taken you *cum grano Salis*-bury.
No wonder Mr. Miall's making merry,
    And rallying his Liberation men—
He sees your tongue so plainly in your cheek,
When in your Church's champion *rôle* you speak.

Go on, neat humbug, laughing in your sleeve.
    And winking, as you bid the Church not falter;
We joy to see her aid from you receive,
    To guard her 'gainst the dangers that assault
        her;
The English Church has had her last reprieve,
    Now *you* are standing boldly by her altar.—
Already in the glass we see the image,
    Of an impending, big religious scrimmage.

DEDICATION.

O, who shall tell the turmoil and the strife—
    The more interminable because religious—
With which the coming Session will be rife,
    When all the rival creeds shall wax litigious,
To help the State keep Madame Church, his wife,
    In proper order? It will be prodigious!
The war of politics becomes mere prattle
Beside a rubrical religious battle.

Thank God! it's coming! we shall live to see
    The State Church crushed, and God from Mammon parted;
England from dowered priestcraft will be free,
    The Bishops from the Upper House all started;
Then flowers and fruit will fill fair wisdom's tree,
    And Superstition from the land be carted.
O, Dizzy, for the coming state of things,
Our muse her warmest thanks, prospective, sings!

The Pope had better dance his *can-cans* straightway,
    For weak-souled Marquises he's proselyted;
See, Truth is mustering at Error's gateway,
    Demanding that the people's wrongs be righted;
Priestcraft is doomed, and this will go a great way
    Tow'rds bringing sunshine into lands benighted.
"The moaning wind"—Oh yes, Ben, we have heard it—
Is rising now, and woe to them that stirred it!

And we, because we call a spade a spade,—
    Despising weak and washy euphemisms,—
Find everywhere false accusations made
    Against us by the smarting "ists" and "isms"

We have attacked ; they like not to be flayed
   O'er fires made up with their own catechisms
So, as they writhe and twist like dying eels,
They make the air resound with libellous squeals.

Some have accused us of a strange design
   Against the Heads and Talès[3] of the land ;
They've traced it in *The Siliad's* ev'ry line,
   And in *The Coming K——* seen treason's brand.
Well, it no way displeases natures fine
   As ours are, when our readers understand
More than we write ; or less, in very truth :
We mean no war ; we've only crossed the Pruth.[4]

To the cool readers of this temp'rate clime,
   Our style of writing may appear erotic ;
But what is ours to Musset's passioned rhyme,
   Or Hugo's shafts 'gainst all that is despotic ?
The nervous English of this modern time
   Will own that in our lines, poor things, is no tic—
'Xcept *douloureux*, perhaps, which brings a pain—
We'll hope we have not giv'n a twinge in vain.

We don't believe, however, in the painful
   Expression worn by some whom we have seen,
Who, speaking of our work, seemed, in the main, full
   Of pimples on their mind, and sought to screen
Impostumations foul, feigning a brainful
   Of purest thoughts, and fancies always clean :
Such people are like blow-flies, who secrete
Their poisoned ova in the freshest meat.

Then there's that cadging dodger, who saw fit
   To write himself down Ass, on scores of pages,
And, in a volume lacking sense or wit,
   To tout for preferment. When next his wages

DEDICATION.

Are paid for such like raids, perhaps he'll hit,
   Or try to hit, the foe that he engages :—
It must be so annoying to lickspittle
   As he did, and be wrong in every tittle.

Go to! you reverend, "lining" gentleman;
   Go, take your 'davies, prostitute your pen;
Go, do your hireling work, as best you can,
   And be, as usual, all things to all men;—
Be high, or broad, or *low*, as suits your plan,
   And, greedily, essay the work of ten;
But, if you've got a spark of manly virtue,
Don't lie again of one who's never hurt you.

Enough of scolding—in our purpose pure,
   We care not what they call us—Fool, or Vandal;
Of good and true souls' approbation sure,
   We glory in the hate of those who brand all
Plain truths as treason; and who can't endure
   That we should lance and probe each public scandal.
The fact being that these purists, who would urge on
Our flaying, need themselves the moral surgeon.

'Tis pleasanter to see that light is spreading,
   That Science has bowled Dogma's middle stump;
And that the rays which Reason's surely shedding,
   Are penetrating now the dense, dark lump
Of Superstition; that fair Truth is heading
   Splay-footed Prejudice, the ugly frump;
That Tyndall's in the van, and naught can turn him—
Oh, wouldn't all the Bigots like to burn him!

Confusion fills the priestly camp; the tocsin
   That called to Church is summoning to Arms;

DEDICATION.

The frightened priests are calling all their flocks in,
   But find they heed no more the ancient charms ;
They vainly, now, are robed their smartest smocks in,
   Their threats and curses fill with no alarms ;
But there they stand, the church's light so dim in,
And find their followers are but fools and women.

Confusion fills the City—Samson's fall
   Has much vexed the financial Philistines ;
And for another unjust judge they call,
   'Stead of King Crump, who crumples their designs,
And is a burden to them, as King Saul
Was to the Israelites. It is hard lines,
No doubt, to find they can nowise ensnare him—
He won't be bought—no wonder they can't " bear" him.

Confusion fills the Country—Tory Squires,
   Elated at their triumph, try to stop
The march of progress, damp down Freedom's fires,
   And ignorance's shaking knees to prop ;
The peasant's child, these worthies say, requires
   No education, he his books must drop—
They care not how degraded their poor neighbour,
Their sole idea is to get cheap labour.

Confusion fills fair France—her breast is torn
   By Royal Sham bores, Bonapartist bullies ;
Her grief is great, and grievous to be borne,
   Her cup of tribulation very full is.
But hope is springing, as she sits forlorn,
   And waits for Fate to move the proper pulleys ;
Her lips shall never an Imperial cub lick,
May she firm found a glorious, free Republic !

The morning comes, the outer darkness breaks,
   And perfect day upon her shall, at last, steal ;
She dreams, and even in her visions shakes
   From her the bloated Bourbon of the Bastile ;
Shrieks, as her hand the young Napoleon takes,
   For at his touch dread mem'ries of the past steal
O'er her ; and, vowing on his race, Vendetta,
She wakes and clings for safety to Gambetta.

And now, we mean to spare your feelings, Ben,
   You're suffering—is it not so ?—from the gout ;
Podagral pains afflict you, so our pen
   Shall show you mercy, and we will not flout
You further—may you soon be well ! and then,
   Why, then, your former mission set about,
Begin again, with resolution hearty,
To educate your stupid Tory party.

Teach it to use its brains, and ears, and eyes,
   Teach it to think that Bigotry's a blunder ;
Teach it that Education is a prize,
   Teach it to hear the moaning wind and thunder,
Teach it to heed the people's warning cries ;
   Teach it to rend the Church and State asunder :
Teach it—but, there, we trust to your sagacity,
For you know best your followers' capacity.

Meantime, Ben Dizzy, we proceed to dedicate,
   In honest, simple verse, our lays to you ;
And though in flattering strains we do not predicate,
   Believe us, our intent is good and true.—
We must our Cantos with a moral medicate
   Because we wish a doctor's work to do :
Our country's sick, we've read the diagnosis,
The knife, applied in time, may save necrosis.

[1] We imply no profane intentions to Mr. Disraeli. He is on the side of the Angels, and, of course, never swears. The "double D." refers merely to that Disendowment and Disestablishment of the English Church, which we rejoice to think, thanks to our Prime Minister, are so imminent.

[2] THING or ALTHING. So was called the first Political Assembly of the Northern nations. To Iceland, many years before the Normans overcame the English, went many thousands of hardy, intelligent settlers from Norway. These were the men who preferred to be damned with all their ancestors, than to be saved without them. Rather than give way to Olaf, who had become a saint, and therefore a persecutor, they elected to depart and seek other shores. Thus, little Iceland became a great community. One Ulfjot was the man for the Thing; the hour was 930, A.D. Thenceforward it met annually on the plains of Thing Valla. For the benefit of our present Premier, who may use the information to serve up in his next Bath Letter, or to his Aylesbury Ordinary Farmers (these yeomen, surely, should be extraordinary ones), when next he addresses them, we shall add one more piece of news. It may be useful to him to know, and to keep in reserve—in company with Wilkes's Extinct Volcanoes, Coningsby's Plundering and Blundering, Balzac's Definition of a Critic, M. Thiers' Obituary Addresses, and the other choice specimens of his talent for eclectic epigrammatizing—that the President of the Thing was called *Lagmadur*. The first syllable is unpleasantly suggestive of the rural *régime*, under which we have the present happiness, according to the received formula, to live, but we trust to the Member for Bucks to keep us moving.

[3] TALES. Suchlike and so distinguished.

See Kinglake's "Crimea;" or the work of any veracious historian of the Russian War, say that of M. Thiers, or, better still, that of any of the companions of the author of the "History of Cæsar."

NOTES TO CANTO THE FIRST.

Our Gentleman from Dauphiny (VIII).—Every public schoolboy knows that the fearless and reproachless Bayard was the grandfather of Chastelard. But, as everybody is not a public schoolboy, we print from the *Dictionnaire de Bouillet* the following brief account of Mary's hapless lover: —"Pierre de Boscobel de Chastelard, un gentilhomme Dauphinois, était petit-fils de Bayard. Ayant conçu une violente passion pour la célèbre Marie Stuart, épouse de Francois II., il suivit cette princesse en Ecosse après la mort de ce monarque. Il fut surpris dans la chambre de Marie, et condamné à perdre la tête." Mr. Swinburne has sung, in impassioned lines, the moving history of Chastelard's erotic adventures; and the *Saturday Review*, whilst rebuking, has fully described them.

David, Bathsheba (XIV).—Mr. Peter Bayle, in his Critical and Historical Dictionary, thus sums up the case he makes against the royal prophet, the man after God's own heart: —"Those who shall think it strange that I speak my mind about the actions of David compared with natural morality, are desired to consider three things:—1. They themselves are obliged to own that the conduct of this prince towards Uriah is one of the greatest crimes which can be committed. There is then only a difference of more or less between them and me; for, I agree with them, that the other faults of the prophet did not hinder him being filled with piety, and great zeal for the glory of God. He was subject alternately to passion and grace. This is a misfortune attending our nature since the fall of Adam. The grace of God very often directed him; but on several occasions passion got the better; policy silenced religion. 2. It is very allowable of private persons, like me, to judge of Facts contained in the Scripture, when they are not expressly characterized by the Holy Spirit. If the Scripture, in relating an action, praises or condemns it, none can appeal from this judgment: every one ought to regulate his approbation or censure on the model of Scripture. I have not acted contrary to this Rule: the facts, upon which I have advanced my humble Opinion, are related in the Holy Scripture, without any mark of approbation affixed by the Spirit of God. 3. It would be doing an injury to the Eternal Laws, and consequently to the true Religion, to give Libertines occasion to object, that when a man has been once inspired by God, we look upon his Conduct as the Rule of Manners; so that we should not dare to condemn the Actions of People, though most opposite to the notions of Equity, when such an one had done them. There is no Medium in this Case; either these actions are not good, or Actions like them are not evil; now, since we must choose either the one or the other, is it not better to take care of the Interests of Morality than the glory of a private Person? Otherwise, will it not be evident, that one chooses rather to expose the Honour of God than that of a mortal Man?

Own the Corn (XVI).—According to the strict classical *ipsissima verba* of the Sacred Védas of the United States, this should be written "acknowledge the corn." Dr. Schele de Vere thus narrates the origin of the phrase. It arose out of the misfortune of a flat-boatman, who had come down to New Orleans, with two flat boats, laden, the one with corn, the other with potatoes. He was tempted to enter a gambling establishment, and lost his money and his produce. On returning to the wharf at night, he found the boat laden with corn had sunk in the river; and when the winner came next morning to demand the stake, he received the answer, "Stranger, *I acknowledge the corn*, take 'em; but the potatoes you *can't* have, by thunder!"

BOOKS AT A DISCOUNT OF 30 TO 75 PER CENT.

S. & T. GILBERT'S NEW CATALOGUE OF VALUABLE BOOKS, offered at the above liberal Discount, is NOW READY, and will be forwarded on application.

S. & T. GILBERT, 36, Moorgate Street, London, E.C.

BOOKS! BOOKS!! BOOKS!!!

THE LARGEST AND BEST SELECTED STOCK OF NEW AND MODERN BOOKS IN LONDON, together with a well-selected Stock of Bibles, Prayer Books, Church Services, Cartes de Visite Albums, &c., &c., conveniently displayed in Show Rooms, and may be viewed without loss of time to the purchaser. The utmost Discount allowed for Cash. Catalogues gratis and postage free.

S. & T. GILBERT, the Original Free Trade and Discount Booksellers,

JON DUAN.

Canto The First.

I.

THE blood of Duan's race was very blue—
  In indigo, indeed, an uncle dealt—
  The Heralds' College, too, had got a clue,
Pursuing which, the prouder members felt
The Duans were as old as any Jew,
  Who had been asked by them to kindly melt
Certain acceptances, from time to time—
As done by Israel in every clime.

II.

The fluid in the Duans' veins was mixed;
  Not wholly Saxon, nor of Norman strain—
For early tribes had not their dwellings fixed,
  But wandered forth in search of grass and grain.
Much as, sweet reader, yesterday, thou picksed
  Thy villa on the Thames, close to the train;—
To mind thy shop in London smoke; then rush
Into the country from the crowd and crush.

III.

The Duans' archives do not throw much light on
  What rank they held, as Cave men, in the past;
But, as their modern way is just to fight on,
  We may suppose they were the men to last;—
That age was not the one to form a Crichton,
  Then were no feeds to speak of, but of mast;
And dinner orat'ry was not in vogue,
Words were so short that all was monologue.

IV.

They searched thro' Lubbock, his Primeval man
  (Whose words weigh well, and far above his coin),
Hoping to find a record of the clan,
  But couldn't trace a single rib or loin
From which they might have come; so chose a bran-
  New pedigree, which sought Jon's folk to join
With one who came with Marie's *suite* from France,
Marie the sweet, who led the men a dance.

V.

All know—a periphrase which means, how few—
  'Mongst Marie's *amants* stood French Chastelard,
Of whom 'tis saying nothing fresh or new,
  That his unfortunate, or lucky, star
Brought her to love him whom she, after, slew;—
  A mangled victim 'neath her loving Car.
But Bayard's grandson felt, when he gained Mary,
Ecstatic bliss, which naught could raise or vary.

VI.

Now, 'tis a very strange, tho' truthful fact,
  That some men, tho' they've known the tip-top dames,
Have not disdained with lowlier maids to act,
  As though the Royal or Imperial flames
Had something in them which so much attacked
  The nerves, that 'spite of the most loyal claims,
They've fell a-flirting with a "Waiting Lady"—
And thought it venial when the Queen was "fadey."

VII.

'Tis certain Chastelard had no excuse
  Of fadiness in Mary, to atone
For making eyes at others, but she deem
  Is in some men, for when they're let alone,
They can't contain themselves; on the loose
  They get; and enter the unfaithful zone
In moment'ry unmindfulness of her
Who, did she know it, would kick up a stir.

VIII.

Our gentleman from Dauphiny had seen
  The Queen's four Maries, and full often thought
Had Mary Stuart not his mistress been,
  One of these dames d'honneur he would have
    sought;
For he had fancy one of them did lean
  A little to his side, when he had brought,
Perchance, some heather from King Arthur's Seat,
To please his Queen, whom he had come to meet.

IX.

And why is it, sweet woman, you incline
  To listen to *his* tongue, and note *his* eye,
And love the fellow, when he isn't thine?
  Is it because you like to make *her* cry,
In whose possession this same youth has lien?
  We fear it is so, and must call "Fie! fie!"
Because, if we don't, others will do 't, you know,
And we, as Jove, had better scold our Juno.

X.

'Twas true enough; one of the four was struck,
  And Chastelard, the striker, had his way;
So well it is to live in way of luck;
  And good such facts, for those who sing the lay—
For, if there were no doe to please the buck,
  No "poor deluded," nor "deceiver gay"—
What would become of novelists and poets,
Tho', for Afflatus' sake, they drank up "Moet's"?

XI.

Have you not heard of Widow Eugénie,
  Who, when a wife, quitting the Emperor,
Did from the Court of France instanter flee,
  And scandal make, because a woman bore
A burden she should not;—one of those *filles*
  Who care for naught but naughtiness, and store
Of di'monds, coral, pearl, and *rentes*, or rolls
Of billets, notes, or cheques on Coutts or Bowles?

XII.

She was a Marguerite, Bellanger to wit,
  Who pleased the Third Napoleon for awhile,
By wiles well known, and for the old well fit—
  These to describe won't suit our English style;
So, by your leave, we would them pretermit,
  Altho' naught pleases more than scenes of guile;
And, to speak truth—which is above and 'fore all—
France is, of all known lands, the most immoral!

XIII.

To Duan's forefathers we would return;
  But must a moment keep you in the South,
To note where Austria's Empress wished to learn
  The English tongue from moustached, warlike
    mouth.
Ah! Francis Joseph, you with rage may burn,
  But, if you won't forsake the ways of youth,
Your charming wife, slim-waisted, full of grace,
Will make *her* game and start a steeple chase.

XIV.

From Dan to Beersheba 'tis all the same :—
  Jacob and Rachel; Sarah and the King;
David, Bathsheba; very much to blame
  (She was a bad mark for the Psalmist's sling);
The tale don't change; 'tis only in the name :
  'Tis not—thank God!—*our* place the dirt to fling,
We leave such work to Beecher and his Church,
Where's dirt enough all Brooklyn to besmirch.

XV.

We hope it's now extremely clear to all
  Where Duan's people came from; for, indeed,
We can't get on without some facts to fall
  Back on; yet, now, some critic who shall read
This verse, may, if permitted, choose to call
  Attention to the fact that our Jon's breed
Is not legitimate, but bastard-born :—
Well, if it must be so,—we'll own the corn.

XVI.

Our first love-making, that's a great event,
  Standing front out the flat shores of our life,
Like Devon sandstone, or chalk cliff in Kent;
  But seldom ending in *her* being our wife,
Whose charms our green youth th' unknown fire
    had lent;
  For boys of eighteen, in their first love-strife,
Find older women more omnipotent
Than younger demoiselles who blush and start,
Not having learned the ways of Cupid's dart.

XVII.

Not more exempt than other white or black man,
  Kalmuck, Caucasian, or wand'ring Tartar,
Or Indian Red, or pig-tail China Jackman—
  Each one for ever wanting some one's "darter"—
Jon felt a shock, and straight became a pack-man
  With a love load, for which he gave in barter
That adoration pure, and worship truthful,
Which *blasé* men sneer down as "very youthful."

XVIII.

Though Duan often laughed at his first hit,
  When harder grown, and much more up to snuff;
Yet, when 'twas on, he felt the strong love-fit
  Shake him with swift sensations, quite enough
To please and torture him, as he did sit
  In admiration mute—the simple muff!—
Of sweet Maria, as she bent her head
Over her book or plate, or prayed, or fed.

XIX.

Like other women who have got to thirty,
  She knew a little of the ways of men,
And, just as happened to our Royal Bertie,
  Duan was taught some things he didn't ken
Before, and found the new-learned ways so "purty,"
  That he became Maria's slave, and ten
Times more than many people thought was proper,
They riding went:—and once Jon came a "cropper."

XX.

'Twas in a hunt down with the West Kent hounds,
  Over the hills, from Horton to the right;
And tho' the pack's not good, and wood abounds,
  Yet 'twas a pretty and exciting sight
To see the horsemen; glorious, too, the sounds
  Of the ground-striking hoofs; fierce, too, the light
Which shone forth from the eyes of those who rode,
Whether they "cock-tails" or well-breds bestrode.

XXI.

Duan was well up in the heated hunt;
  The huntsman blew his horn, and o'er the plough,
With varying speed came, with a snort or grunt,
  Chesnuts and bays; and Duan made a vow
The Brush he'd have; but saw he'd have to shunt
  One fellow, who was just before him now,
Going like steam, and clearly not inclined
To yield his place to anyone behind.

XXII.

The hill is breasted, and the top is reached,
  And fast down hill the line of hounds extends;
And to the yokel old, and boy just breeched,
  Who stand beneath the hedge, just where it bends,
It is a view superb; and 'twill be preached
  That night, in slow Kent phrase, which greatly tends
To help the tale:—that "'twor a real bloomin'
Soight to see the hounds over plough a-coomin'."

XXIII.

Lady Maria is but gently moving,
  She knows the paces; knows, too, the wire fences;
And tho' her temperament's inclined to loving,
  She's found that common sense the topping sense is;
So she reserves herself, but keeps improving
  The place she has; but never once commences
To try her very best, till she's persuaded
She must try other charms, since youth's are faded.

XXIV.

In following foxes, she was just the same,
  She was as cool at this as when a heart
Was startled by her eyes; or other game,
  On which she'd set her mind, was in the mart;
Nor cruel, nor selfish was she, but a dame
  Ready on any jig or joust to start;
And loved that man who near at hand did lay,
To take her to the field or to the play.

XXV.

Now Duan suited her just to a "t,"
  Except in this—he was a trifle young;
That didn't matter for a *vis-à-vis*,
  But in the hunting field, it might be flung
Into her face, by a dear, kind lady
  (Thus Charity adorns the female tongue),
That she had brought her nephew out from Eton,
Where, probably, he had been lately beaten.

XXVI.

She knew that Duan loved her, but she'd passed—
  Like nearly all who are *bon-ton*, just now—
Through such experiences in years amassed,
  That she well knew the value of a vow

Made by a youth to her who's aging fast;—
  She knew some day or other they would "row."
Were there not hidden in her books and drawers,
  Portraits of lovers she had lost by scores?

XXVII.

But if we slowly canter in this way,
  Searching my Lady's mind, the night will come,
And find our hunters, after a hard day,
  Distant a weary twenty miles from home.
So that we catch Jon Duan, let us pray—
  And, as it's heavy going on wet loam,
We'll spur our Pegasus with hopes of laurel;
And pass the field of horses, bay and sorrel.

XXVIII.

In the best families, accidents occur;
  And hunting accidents are never rare;
Think of the chances: you may catch your spur,
  Cannon your enemy, or throw your mare:
In many such ways you may make a stir,
  And at a county meeting gain a stare,
From some sweet creature, who, like Desdemona,
Loves hair-breadth 'scapes as well as *Dea bona*.

XXIX.

Duan's last gallop was almost performed,
  Although he'd no idea of what was coming;
And, as veracious poets, well informed,
  We should not merit praises, but a drumming
Out of the Laureate's fort so late we stormed,
  If we delayed from saying, that the numbing
Sensations Duan's just experiencing
Were not due to ill riding, or bad fencing.

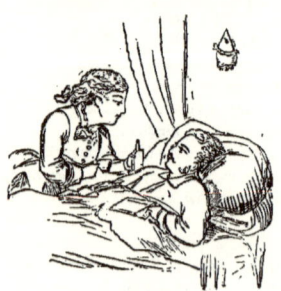

XXX.

For 'twas no fence he'd gone at, nor drop jump,
  Nor anything that tries a horseman's skill;
And tho' some roarers had begun to pump,
  Through having gone the pace that's sure to kill
The duffers; yet Jon's mare, a thorough trump,
  Went steady, as an old 'un at a mill;
So we must tell you in the following strain,
Why Duan lay extended on the plain.

XXXI.

For him, as many others, 'twas a drain
  That settled him; a drain too much, in fact,
Which had been made to carry off the rain,
  But sent our hero spinning—a worse act,

Causing, perhaps, concussion of the brain ;
So sudden and so shocking the impact.
For Duan's mare, alas, put her foot in it,
And Duan's head came "crack," in half a minute.

XXXII.

Our hero lay there very much at rest ;
  The blood oozed from his temple, o'er his eye ;
And all his get-up, hat and coat and vest,
  Was sadly soiled ; and some said he would die
Before assistance came ; which added zest
  To the day's sport ; though some might haply cry,
When they did hear their favourite was killed,
Upon a field not warlike, but just tilled.

XXXIII.

Not many stopped to see what could be done :
  A hunt is not the place for sentiment ;
Those for'ard didn't want to lose the fun,
  And were on Reynard's death much more intent,
Than caring for the life of any one
  As human as themselves ; quite innocent
Of any motive, yet no doubt believing
The world would be improved by some men leaving.

XXXIV.

But we will do some justice while we may,—
  And, *place aux dames*, my Lady gallops up
On her old grey, well warranted to stay
  The longest run, and ready aye to sup
On his bran mash at close of hardest day ;
  Welcomed at home by stable cat and pup,—
Lady Maria joins the little group,
Nor lets, on seeing Jon, her courage droop.

XXXV.

Forth from her flask a little spirit pours
  Into our hero's mouth ; his poor pale lips
Reminding her of kisses by the scores
  She'd had of them ; such as a woman sips,
Who's fond of kissing, and, in fact, adores
  The men who give them ; 'twas her ladyship's
Delight, indeed ; and we repeat once more,
She'd plenty had from other men before.

XXXVI.

Duan's white brow she bandaged like a Sister
  Of Charity, or like a St. John's nurse,
With her own handkerchief, while, to assist her,
  A little sporting doctor—none the worse
That he the chase loved well as pill and blister—
  Felt Duan's pulse; and said, "There'll be no hearse
Wanted for him this bout, if common care
Is taken, but he's bound to lose his hair."

XXXVII.

He'd lost his fox, and now must lose his hair,
  'Twas very hard ; at least it seemed hard lines ;
But, then, you see, he'd gained a something there
  Which they knew not ; for Providence combines
A set of compensations, and don't spare
  For lenience e'en to sinners' faults and fines ;
Content if of good deeds she find a few—an'
There really was a lot of good in Duan.

XXXVIII.

Two "varmer's" men upon a hurdle took him,
  Gently as if he'd been their little child,
To a near cottage, nor at all they shook him ;
  For little food had made their natures mild.
And Lady May not for an inch forsook him,
  But on his handsome face, all-hoping, smiled.
It is quite true—if you'd a woman win,
Get weak or wounded, then you will "wire in."

XXXIX.

With more of tender feeling than she'd felt
  For Duan all the time that he had courted her,
My Lady, self-controlled, unused to melt,
  Smiling most sweetly just when things most thwarted her,
Having the nature of the happy Celt—
  (Debrett and Burke of Irish blood reported her)—
My Lady led the way for Duan's entry,
And, as the yokels bore him in, stood sentry.

XL.

The cottage was a lovely little place,
  Belonging to my lord, we mean not ours, but
Lady Maria's lord, who had the grace,
  Being a kind lord—blessed, too, with the "Gower" strut—
To be quite blind to the most obvious trace
  Of 'Ria's "goings on," e'en in her bower shut ;
Nor cared a jot for what was said by rumour,
As long as Lady M. kept in good humour.

XLI.

We hope we're clear before our readers now—
    We've had a deal of trouble with the rhyme;
We've landed Duan, who will make his bow
    As soon as may be, in his gaysome prime;
Cured of his wound;—but, there, we don't know how
    His heart will feel; still, loving is no crime,
And we, with all our hearts, wish Duan joy,
Having become quite spooney on the boy.

XLII.

And sweet on him, my Lady came—Eheu!
    'Tis ever so; one gives the cheek to kiss,
The other kisses it: we know it, so do you:
    Duan before his fall had felt the bliss
Of loving; now, somehow, he'd lost the cue,
    Whilst Lady May had found how much she'd miss
When Duan should depart; but in her cooings,
She never once deplored her present doings.

XLIII.

Is that a fact about remorse, we wonder?
    Is it the least true that men do repent
When youth and age lie many years asunder,
    And all our brightness and our force are spent?—
Grieve men for youthful follies as a blunder?—
    Is sackcloth worn for salad merriment?—
It may be so; still we think, indigestion
Alone makes men say "Yes" to such a question.

XLIV.

We've known a many various men in life,
    High, Low, Jack, Game, all four, all sorts and sizes;
Some who've behaved like bricks in serious strife,
    Some on the bench, some summon'd to th' assizes,
One's in the Church, one's just divorced his wife,
    And one's a publisher, who advertises
What he declares is "Beeton's Annual New,"
Whilst B. asserts the statement isn't true.

XLV.

Being inquisitive, that we might know
    From diff'rent minds what each felt on this point,
We've asked the men above if it is so
    With them, if they regretted any joint

Proceedings in those sweet spring days, that go
So swift and are so precious, that anoint
With pungent memories all the years that follow,
When baldness comes, and teeth are growing
    hollow.

XLVI.

Well, each one's answer show'd the self-same thing,
  Which was, that they'd enjoyed their youth-time
    greatly,
And that the only trouble and real sting
  Was, in some cases, that they'd grown too
    stately—
(Which meant, too fat) that no new times could bring
  The pleasures of the past;—when Bridget,
    "nately,"
Would dance a jig, Janet the Highland Fling,
Rose fill the cup, and Alice ditties sing.

XLVII.

Ah! dear old Béranger has caught the strain—
  "*La jambe bien faite et le temps perdu*,"
Never such honest verse we'll see again ;
  For, readers (this betwixt ourselves and you),
Humbug has on this land such strong chains lain,
  We ne'er, with all our strength, can break them
    through,
Until—oh ! happy day, arise ! arise !—
Truth makes Hypocrisy her lawful Prize.

XLVIII.

'Twas most important you should understand
  Our feelings on the subject of Remorse,
Because the subject that we have in hand—
  (That it's objective, Bismarck would enforce)
Duan, the subject, is of that stout band
  Who nothing but the natural, will endorse;
And, as we can't be fighting our own hero,
We "ditto" say, though Cant may weep, "Oh,
    dear, oh!"

XLIX.

As Duan, soon, became a little better,
  And his hurt temple had begun to heal ;
He learnt how much he was my Lady's debtor,
  And with his thanks, and more, soon made her
    feel
How sweet caresses are ; and thinking, set her,
  How grateful manhood is ; and set the seal
Of real fervour on the yielding wax,
Which, when not felt, makes loving limp and lax.

L.

These cottage days, alas, too quickly fled ;
  And ever more my Lady treasured them ;
For, though she gaily spent her time, and led,
  In after life, the rout, nor sought to stem
Her later fancies, when Jon's love was dead—
  Yet, when they met, it needed all her phlegm
To seem as though she'd never cared about him,
And had but nursed, in order just to flout, him.

LI.

One day a maiden, urged by anguish keen,
  Went down by the North Kent to Greenhithe
    Station,
For in her Western home she had just seen—
  Amongst the other news of our great nation—
Duan's mishap described, and how he'd been
    Thought dead. She, in a loving perturbation,
Did not clap spurs into her steed, as knights would,
But left by the first train which called at Brites-
    wood.

LII.

Lady Maria had gone up to town,
  To be at Guelpho's fancy ball that night :
So, met the train which brought the damsel down.
  We'll not go in for telling the brave sight
At Marlborough House—but note the inquiring
    frown
  My Lady's maid gave, as she asked "What
    might
Miss want with Mister Jon—he's very weak,
And doctor has left word he mustn't speak?"

LIII.

Poor Letty Lethbridge, she was near to faint,
  When the trained maid thus met her anxious
    quest ;
But love is strong in sinner and in saint,
  And to see Jon she still would do her best :—
"Is there no way to see him ?"—"No, there ain't,"
  The Cockney said.—"I won't disturb his rest,"
Said pretty Letty,—"Only just to see him ;
Oh, won't the doctor let me, if I fee him ?"

LIV.

"Fee *him*, indeed ! If anyone could do it,
  I am the party, although *I* dare not.
My Lady, on the spot, would make me rue it."
  "Lady !—what lady?," Letty gasped, all hot.

Lady Maria; if she only knew it,
  She'd give up Coming K—— and all the lot;
My goodness me! it puts me in a tremyor
  Only to think of it! what a dilemyor!"

LV.

Billings was yielding; only just a little,
  But 'twas enough to give the Lethbridge hope,—
Not that my Lady's maid did care a tittle
  About my Lady's anger: she could cope
With that; besides, she knew how very brittle
  Was man's love, and how soon and sharp it broke;
And she had seen some symptoms of Jon's tiring,
And thought *his* would go out, bar some new firing.

LVI.

Letty began then, in a gracious way—
  She had her purse, too, in her open palm:—
"I want to see Jon Duan, and I pray
  You do whate'er you can to bring me balm;
And I will give you all I have, to-day,
  If but my fears about him I may calm.
Let me but have one peep at him, sweet honey,
And you shall have—oh, lots and lots of money!"

LVII.

The sovereigns did it—Letty gave her purse,
  And Billings took her where our hero lay,
Saying, "You mustn't make a bit of 'furse,'
  Then I don't mind how long you with him stay."
And Letty, happy she was now his nurse,
  Felt that her night had brightened into day,
Though, still, the jealous doubt would come to bother,
Who was this lady, whom she longed to smother?

LVIII.

Duan was dozing; men do, ill or well;
  And nothing's more enjoyable on earth,
Whether you're visioning the last night's belle
  You danced with; or when comes a total dearth
Of news and scandal. So that it befell
  Letty did gaze, as Duan dozed. No berth
So pleasurable could anyone have given her—
To write down all her joy, 'twould take a scrivener.

LIX.

Duan, in turning lazily about,
  Opened his peepers, and caught sight of something
Which, to his half-roused mind, did seem, no doubt,
  A little strange; however, like a dumb thing,
He stayed; and baby-like, tried to make out
  What 'twas before his eyes—a fee, fo, fum thing,
His doziness divined;—soon, shape it takes,
And when it did so, quickly Duan wakes.

LX.

We're not a Wilkie Collins—God be praised!
  Not that we don't think involutions fine;
We do, in fact; but don't wish our brain crazed
  To trace a tale in geometric line.
So don't imagine you are to be mazed
  Just after, or before, you've been to dine—
For 'twas indeed a simple, plain old thing
That Duan saw—a palpable gold ring.

LXI.

That plain gold rings resemble plain gold rings,
  Must be, we think, a proposition simple—
It would not puzzle one of our old kings;
  Still, there is many a woman with a dimple,
Whose nerves are sensitive on such old things;
  And e'en that sister, who doth wear a wimple,
Is touched, maybe, when those smooth circlets golden
Are seen on hands where they should not be holden.

LXII.

But as a cheese-mite knows another mite,
  In that rich Stilton cheese you have in cut;
And as an oyster knows its pearl by sight,—
  So Duan knew this ring from out a rut
Of rings; and would have bet, e'en being "tight,"
  He'd spot it in whatever light 'twas put;
For 'twas the one he'd put on Letty Lethbridge
One day at church, when they were down at Fettridge.

LXIII.

Poor little Robson in that wondrous rôle
  Of wand'ring Minstrel, which he really made,—
Unlike creations now, which most are "stole,"—
  When he did sing of Villikins's jade,
Was wont to pause, as he his song did troll,
  And, looking with that look demurely staid,
Would say, 'Tis not a comic song I'm singing—
So we—'Tis not an intrigue we're beginning.

Fair Fancy at the West.—The Coming K——'s Ball.

LXIV.

There's nothing on the cross, we do assure you,
  No figure of the kind you'll see in Spain ;—
We don't invent bad stories to allure you,
  We leave such things for Ouida to explain.
Duan's a gentleman, and is to cure you
  Of some crude notions as to future pain ;
Meanwhile, there's something in the following stanza,—
  At least we'll hope so, and say—Esperanza !

LXV.

Now for it ; let us tell about the ring—
  'Tis not the Book and Ring, remember that ;
But just a story of a boy in spring,
  Who gave his play and pew-mate, pink and fat,
This rounded circlet, whose romance we sing,
  Causing amongst her fellows mirth and chat,
Whene'er they met at Manor House or Farm—
Now where, ye nasty nice ones, where's the harm?

LXVI.

If you are disappointed, Tartuffe olden,
  So much the better ; you have bought our poem,
Hoping for some things you'll not find so golden—
  Or gilded, rather, as you hoped we'd show 'em—
You've bought J. D., and carefully it folden
  In that same drawer with pictures where you stow 'em ;
And now you're done—we're very glad to do you,
And if we could—you and your crew, we'd stew you !

LXVII.

But all this time we've purposely abstained
  From peeping at Jon Duan and his Letty ;
We know she's thoroughly by spot unstained,
  And think that looking on is very petty,
So is eavesdropping ; and if you are pained,
  Good-hearted reader, kiss your own dear Betty ;
And you will know, for one thing, what they did,
Although we were not 'hind the curtains hid.

LXVIII.

Thanks to his nature fine, a well-bred man
  Will reverence what is good and what is pure ;
He mayn't believe what's told of prophet Dan,
  'Nor many things of which the Pope's cock-sure,
Yet will he carry out what he began ;
  His love of truth for truth's sake will endure ;
You'll always find he's hard upon the pious,—
Who, if they could, would burn us, and then try us.

LXIX.

Sweet, simple Letty, she was very charming,
  Such a good little thing, that all did love her ;
And as for anyone to think of harming
  Her, 'twas impossible ; for those above her,
And those in rank below, who did the farming
  Upon her father's land, would ever cover her
With blessings for her kind and thoughtful ways,
And give her, what the parson wanted—praise.

LXX.

Duan had seen not much of London town,
  Before he scented something dull and vapid,
And though he was too young, as yet, to frown
  On those who set the pace a little rapid,
Yet, for all that, he often took a train down
  To see the little maid he ne'er found sapid ;
Who, though, o'erjoyed to see her darling lover,
Took time before she could her wits recover.

LXXI.

If you know such a maiden, and are young,
  Love her and bless her, keep your troth and word ;
Not all the songs that poets ever sung,
  Not all the sweetest trills from singing-bird,
Not Shelley's lark, nor linkèd sweetness flung
  By Swan of Avon,—sweetest sounds e'er heard ;
Not all these, on a million others mounted,
Can claim an ear, when a maid's tale's recounted.

LXXII.

We've not a word to say for Duan's flirting
  With other women in his London life ;
He couldn't be accused, 'tis true, of hurting
  The sentiments so dear to Grundy's wife,
His *bonnes fortunes* he never thought of blurting ;
  No cuckold threatened him with shot or knife ;
No more discreet young fellow's gone to Hades
In what concerned his doings with the ladies.

LXXIII.

My Lady knew that Duan was a leal lad,
  But that he loved like *Jeunesse* loved the L'Enclos,
A *petite passion*, which makes one feel mad
  For a few weeks or months, but doesn't often go

Longer than that ; then one feels hard and steel-
    clad
'Gainst her who might have nursed you in
    your long clo'—
Old women can't expect men's love for ever,
Let them, of all wiles that they know, endeavour.

LXXIV.

It had all passed—his heart was wholly Letty's ;
    Just now at any rate, and he forgot
The hunting and the fall, for he had met his
    First love, won in past years, whom not for dot
He loved ; for by the side of Lady Betty's,
    The Lethbridge lands were small and mort-
        gaged—not
Like neighbouring Lady B.'s, who owned the park,
But hadn't quite the charms to please our spark.

LXXV.

The day had worn on ; Duan had been served
    With all his usual fare, and Letty went
At times to see the walks and roads that curved
    Around the cottage built on an ascent,
Commanding a grand view, which well deserved
    The title of the prettiest scene in Kent—
There down below, seen through its oaks and
    beeches,
Stretched Father Thames down to the sea in
    reaches.

LXXVI.

They'd spoken of old times, our youth and maid,
    And smiled and laughed, and Letty nearly
        cried
At the remembrance of a cruel thing said
    By Duan once. She'd been, too, sorely tried,
When older girls made eyes at Jon ;—afraid
    That he might change, and take another bride.
But Duan's just that "kinder sort o' man," you
    see,
Who knows the sex as well as Ballantyne, Q.C.

LXXVII.

He might make blunders in the books he pub-
    lished,
    Be an enthusiast for Rochefort's *Lanterne;*
Be in a bargain with Barabbas vanquished
    (Jon in mere trading was the wee-est bairn) ;

But with the women ne'er was Duan dubbed
    " dished "—
    As Derby dished the Whigs—but like Jules
        Verne,
Takes Phileas round the world in eighty days,
Duan the women won ; he knew their ways.

LXXVIII.

He had a funny theory on this head,
    Which may be worth reporting to the world
(If it is not, just think, then, 'twas not said).
    Well, his assertion was, that hair which curled,
Bright eyes which shone (and weren't like cod-
    fish dead),
    Long arms that clasped as in the waltz they
        twirled,
The lissom limb, the backbone straight, and
    small feet,
Were manly charms which in most men don't all
    meet.

LXXIX.

And when they did,—and here you'll see the
    point,—
    Women admired, and common men did hate
The lucky man who showed the shapely joint :
    And in this life 'twas sure to be his fate
That all the sex that's fair would him anoint
    With sweetest unguents, morning, noon, or
        late—
And so it worked, that men who'd luck with
    women,
Had usually to count most males their foemen.

LXXX.

Poor Letty had been hovering round the question
    As to the lady of whom Billings spoke ;
And she had often got as far as " Yes, Jon,
    But tell me who ?"—and then her courage
        broke.
She was afraid, perhaps, of his digestion,
    And more she feared that she might be awoke
To listen to some fearful revelation,
More shocking than poor Lady Dilke's cremation.

LXXXI.

Well, and it came at last, and Duan felt it
    A very awkward question to discuss ;
But, the bull taking by the horns, he dealt it
    A blow which settled it without much fuss :

He knew the girl's soft heart, and so, to melt it,
  He told her all about his absent "nuss";
Except a fact or two, by some suspected,
  At which poor Letty might have felt dejected.

LXXXII.

But we have left Society some time,
  And how will that great mart get on without us?
To-day a hundred would commit a crime
  To gain an entry—pray, will any doubt us?—
To see the Coming K——'s great pantomime
  At Marlborough House; and, oh, how some will flout us
Because we print—what some there dared to say—
  "We wonder if Lorne's mother-in-law will pay?"

LXXXIII.

A change of scene now comes; and for a spell,
  Whilst Duan's getting happier every minute,
We go to town, and cab it to Pall Mall,
  And see the world, and hear what fresh news' in it;—
And there's a story going, which, if no sell,
  Bodes mischief; so we may as well begin it:—
Lady Maria, 'spite of phlegm and fashion,
Has gone into a fearful, towering passion.

LXXXIV.

A Duchess, agèd, one of Guelpho's friends,
  Met her at Madame Louise's to-day;
And—see how small a thing the sex offends—
  Asked if her little boy went out to play.
Furious, on Duchess M. a frown she bends,
  Retorting—"Now, be careful what you say,
Or I shall tell that little tale of Bertie,
When he was but sixteen and you were thirty."

LXXXV.

This shocked the Duchess very much, perhaps;
  But, with the *sang froid* of a lady born,
She said, "You go to Marlborough House, of course,
  To-night; you'll be received just like poor Lorne:
You'll see if Guelpho will my words endorse,
  For all your life your words to me you'll mourn."
Then spoke to Madame Louise as to lace,
Without the least emotion in her face.

LXXXVI.

Lady Maria did not stay to buy
  What she intended for the ball that night;
She knew how useless 'twas her wit to try,
  And 'gainst her Grace's influence to fight;
So unto Duan's arms she thought she'd fly,
  And tell her sorrows to her youthful knight.
Alas! her cup was soon to overflow,
And she was doomed to feel a harder blow.

LXXXVII.

A woman's senses are extremely keen,
  When she's in love, and Letty heard some words
Spoken below, and ere the form was seen,
  She knew, as know the little mother birds
When danger threatens—there must be a scene;
  And, as a warrior his armour girds,
So Duan's present nurse her courage braces,
Nor shows of fear even the slightest traces.

LXXXVIII.

Having within us tender hearts and pity,
  We feel grief for the elder woman's case;
We're not like those promoters in the City,
  Who laugh at victims of their schemings base;
We feel that Duan's conduct's not been pretty,
  And that he don't deserve an ounce of grace;
But, having said so in our own defence,
We'll let the ladies show their skill of fence.

LXXXIX.

Duan sat up upon his sofa, thinking,
  As on the stairs my Lady's foot-fall fell,
Whoever got the best in the sharp pinking,
  He could not come out of the contest well;
There was no way of skulking or of blinking;
  In fact, he felt quite sea-sick at the swell
Of varying emotions, which, like ocean's,
Caused heavings tremulous and nauseous motions.

XC.

Entered, the practised woman of the world,
  To tread the stage, and act a scene of life;
Her look was thunder, scorn her pale lips curled,
  A very Amazon, arrayed for strife;
At Letty, epithets like javelins hurled,
  Piercing the maiden's bosom like a knife;
Yet, past the understanding of our dull wit,
She said no word against the real culprit.

XCI.

Letty grew fierce, as Duan's heart was wrung;
  She, with the divination purely sexual,
Knew why the taunts at her alone were flung;
  And, though there's no description that's called textual,

Of every fierce and horrid phrase that stung ;
    Yet, women-folk, though we, so writing, vex
        you all,
Believe that if Jon had been absent, then,
The work would have been different for our pen.

XCII.

'Twas jealousy of Letty's being there—
    There, in the very room for Jon made nice,
By her (Maria's) loving hands and care—
    Proved, 'neath the smooth exterior, there was
        vice—
Vice like you found in that neat chesnut mare,
    Which, bucking freely, threw you, fairly, thrice :
Vesuvian slopes, which vines and verdure drape,
Hide furious fires which, one day, must escape.

XCIII.

Letty, whose temper had been growing heated
    Under the bellows of my lady's rage,
Now moved from where Jon lately had been seated,
    Just like a frigate going to engage :
" Madam, you have me in a manner treated
    Quite unbecoming to your rank and age ;
I felt to Duan as to a dear brother,
And he tells me *you* 've been to him a mother.

XCIV.

" Why, therefore, Madam, anger should you show,
    Because I came to see him, having read,
Altho' the news had travelled very slow,
    He'd had a fall, and had been left for dead ;
Why was I wrong in setting forth to know
    If there was truth in what the papers said ?
Jon Duan is my own accepted lover,
Why should I from the world my true love cover ?

XCV.

Potent is truth, and potent, too, is candour—
    The latter may be now and then excessive,
As in some lines of Walter Savage Landor ;
    But there was nothing wrong, or too aggressive,
In Letty's words ; for she was bound to stand or
    Fall by faith in Duan—who, digressive
From virtuous paths, should be received with
    more joy,
Than if he'd always been an honest, poor boy.

XCVI.

The moment came, and with it came the man ;
    It was too much for Duan to rest longer ;
So, gathering his strength, he thus began :
    " I would not wish in any way to wrong her,
Who's been so kind to me ; and when I scan
    The kindness of her ladyship, feel stronger
To declare I shall remain for life her debtor,
And that no woman could be kinder, better ;

XCVII.

" Still, and with shame I am obliged to own it,
    However kindly Lady May has nursed me,
My loyalty is due, where I've not shown it,—
    To Letty Lethbridge ; for, cruel fate has
        cursed me
With a weak nature—oh ! how I bemoan it—
    Which has brought grief to you two, and
        immersed me
In what I thoroughly deserve—a slough of des-
    pond—
'Twould serve me right if some one said a
    horse-pond."

XCVIII.

But it avails not to prolong the view
    Of this unhappy meeting of the three ;
'Tis better to get each out of the stew
    As best we can ; and Duan will agree
He'd rather be one of a Lascar crew
    Under a Yankee "boss," or "up a tree," ;
Or be in any sort of bad condition,
Than stay in that room, in his then position.

XCIX.

So plucking up his courage and his strength,—
    " Lady Maria, I will take my leave,"
He said ; and saying, rose, erect, full length,—
    " Miss Lethbridge," turning to the girl, " I
        grieve
That my misconduct should (here a parenth-
    Esis occurred from failing breath)—I grieve
I have occasioned so much pain to friends—
I will do all I can to make amends."

C.

And bowing " farewell " to her ladyship—
    As, with a courtesy, Letty went out too,—
Duan, with faltering step and many a " trip,"
    Passed down the stairs, and then the door
        went through,
Into the grounds, where to his trembling lip
    Came from the beating heart, " Thank God,
        I do,
That *that* is over." So do we sincerely ;
The printers, too, whose patience we've tried,
    dearly.

Canto The Second.

I.

WE sing our Court—select, sedate, demure,
    Bound in the virtuous chains Victoria forges ;
So good, so dull, so proper, and so pure,
And O ! so different from her Uncle George's—
That "first of gentlemen," who, it seems sure,
    Was fond of "life" and bacchanalian orgies ;
That blood relation of " our kings to be,"
Who did not spell his " quean" with double " e."

II.

How great the change ! the courtly newsman's pen
    Has never now to rise above the level
Of commonplace particulars, save when
    Victoria in her Highland home holds revel,
And dances with her Scotch dependents then,
    As though she'd learned the castanets at Seville—
Not that with such vivacity we quarrel—
But why does she confine it to Balmoral ?

III.

We wish our Queen would dance a little more,
    Would follow Queen Elizabeth's example ;
And of her powers upon the dancing-floor
    Would give us Englishmen, down south, a sample.
That Scots alone are favoured makes us sore,
    For surely London loyalty's as ample :
And, with all deference, we think it silly
To dance a reel with gamekeeper or gillie.

IV.

How " Good Queen Bess " danced, history relates—
    You find it in her memoirs by Miss Aikin,
" High and disposedly" she danced, as states
    Quaint Sir James Melvil, who was somewhat shaken
By what he saw ; and yet we find by dates
    Her age then may at twenty-nine be taken—
A by no means too great age for a maiden
To dance, although with Queenly duties laden.

V.

And yet the people talked, and wagged their chins,
    To hear the English Church's head was dancing ;[1]
But now, when England's Sovereign begins
    To step it—*vide* note[2]—we're not romancing—

We're rather glad, nor care a pair of pins,
  Though she in years is certainly advancing;
But, as we've said, its only right and fair,
  Royal partners should be picked out with more care.

VI.

When, too, our virgin monarch ruled the land
  (And, by the way, there's doubt of her virginity),
She showed for certain nobles, great and grand,
  A manifest and somewhat warm affinity;
And favourites ruled her Court, we understand,
  And queenly heart as well, and the divinity
That hedges kings and queens—see Shakspeare's plays—
Was at a discount, rather, in those days.

VII.

Now quite another scene is being enacted
  (Our Queen has morals far above suspicion),
And quite another way our Sovereign's acted,
  A way not wholly fitting her position;—
For now the British public's ear's attracted
  By circumstantial tales of the admission
Of menial Scotchmen to the royal favour;—
This does not of the regal instinct savour.

VIII.

Cophetua loved a beggar-maid, 'tis true,
  But that was passion, love has some excuse;
But how excuse the Sovereign who can view
  A set of stalwart gillies, *sans* the trews,
With what we call a preference undue?
  Not that our Lady has no right to choose,
But—wishing to be loyally obedient,—
We still assert such friendship's not expedient.

IX.

If she'd have councillors, and friends, and guides,
  Let her choose them 'mongst British gentlemen;
And not select them from Scotch mountain-sides,
  Nor pick them from the crofter's smoky den;
Nor trust the adventurers Germany provides,
  Nor furnish tattle for the reckless pen
By efforts vain—the adage old and terse is—
To make the sow's ears into silken purses.

X.

It is not seemly that the servants' hall
  Should form a Court, nor that the servants there
Should be the sole *invités* to a ball
  Which the Queen graces with her presence rare;

Nor that she only hold high carnival
  When her Scotch servants marry; 'tis not fair
To us, who royal smiles are never rich in,
To find them lavished freely on her kitchen.

XI.

It may be pleasing, in a way, to hear
  The luck of Ballater, and Bræmar Glen;
How there our Sovereign for half the year
  Retires from midst the haunts of Englishmen,
And spends her morning, dropping the sad tear,
  And building Albert cairns on every Ben—
Then courts reaction in the afternoons,
By hearing Willie Blair play Scottish tunes.

XII.

Or taking tea in some dependent's cottage,
  Or seeing poor old widow Farquharson,
Or sharing some 'cute Highland woman's pottage,
  Or choosing for a gillie her stout son;—
But such things smack a "wee" too much of dotage,
  To make us happy when we hear they're done;
We want our Queen, in whom such duties rests,
To come and entertain her *Rôyal* guests.

XIII.

Come, if you please, Victoria, do not waste
  Your valued time 'midst stalwart grooms and keepers,—
We dare not question your most royal taste,
  Or we would add, cut off the "widow's weepers,"—
Come back to us to do your duties, haste;
  And leave old memories among the sleepers;
And if for quiet you still sometimes burn,
Let Ireland, long-neglected, have its turn.

XIV.

Nor make the Crathie church a raree-show,
  To which the enterprising landlords run
Post-chaises, omnibuses, to and fro,
  Crowded with tourists eager for the fun
Of scrambling for the places whence they know
  A good view of their Sovereign may be won—
And, in a spirit less devout than jocular,
Their eyesight aid with Dollond's binocular.

XV.

They turn their backs on altar and on preacher,
  For the best pews with golden bribes they treat,
Regardless of the words of our great Teacher—
  "Make not My house a money-changer's seat!"—

Forgetting God, they gaze up at his creature.
   Your Majesty, this, surely, is not meet:—
Then they slip out as soon as they are able,
   And make the tombstones serve as luncheon-table.

XVI.

O, stop this crying scandal, if you please,
   Encourage not this sacrilege so shocking;
Let not the tourists push, and rush, and squeeze,
   Like London roughs to play-house gallery flocking;
Nor let next summer bring such scenes as these,
   All that is sacred so completely mocking.
It can on no pretence be right and proper, a
House of God should be "Her Majesty's Opera!"

XVII.

What is there in stern Caledonia's air
   That makes our Sovereign forget her grief?
We wish profoundly she'd conceal her care
   From English subject as from Scottish fief.
For we be loyal too, and cannot bear
   The Gael should solely give our Queen relief—
That Highland pibrochs should her joys enhance,
Whilst we pipe on in vain to make her dance.

XVIII.

Surely would sing all England a *Te Deum*
   If she could her beloved Queen persuade
To lock for once and all the Mausoleum,
   To leave in peace the dear, departed shade;
Be less the *égoïste*, think less of "meum,"
   Save hard-worked ministers, and commerce aid,
By ending her seclusion;—and to lean,
Being still a woman, to be more a Queen!

XIX.

We know her virtues—how she drives and walks,
   And goes to church with charming regularity;
We know her business tact—how well she talks
   On politics; we know her gracious charity
To German poverty—('tis true, want stalks
   In Osborne Cottages: why this disparity
We cannot say, though surely what is right
In Gotha, 's ditto in the Isle of Wight).

XX.

We know, we say, how very pure our Queen is,
   And what a manager! and what a mother!
But, though all this so very plainly seen is,
   We cannot quite our discontentment smother.
Her virtues we admire;—but what we mean is,
   Of two moves she should choose the one or t'other:—
The one is—Coming out amongst the nation;
The other—Going in for Abdication.

XXI.

'Tis give and take. If we continue loyal—
   And we are so without the slightest doubt—
We certainly expect our lady royal
   Will keep a court, and not aye fret and pout,—
Water without a fire will cease to boil,
   And loyalty unshone on may go out.
If shining on it is not in her line,
Then let the Son appear and have a shine!

XXII.

We do not pay our Sovereign to hide
   In northern solitudes, however sweet;
We want to view her in her pomp and pride,
   And cheer her in the park and in the street;
We want her in our midst and at our side,
   To grace our triumphs and our joys complete.
It does not seem a dignified position
To put Great Britain's sceptre in commission.

XXIII.

Our Royal Mistress, yet, should have her due,—
   She did come up to town a bit last season;
May she, next year, again, that course pursue,
   And longer stay—we trust this is not treason—
Indeed, we personally yield to few
   In loyalty; and therein lies the reason
Why on her Gracious Majesty we call
To heed the handwriting upon the wall.

XXIV.

Well, as we've said, last season saw the Queen
   In London; and, most marvellous to say,
Whilst she was ling'ring sadly on the scene,
   She held a drawing-room *herself* one day:
And, naturally, with ardour very keen,
   Our fairest rushed their compliments to pay.
Duan, of course, as in his bounden duty,
Was in attendance at the beck of beauty.

XXV.

He wish'd, *sans doute*, that beauty had *not* beckon'd,
   For drawing-rooms were not in Duan's line,—
Most etiquette insuff'rable he reckon'd,
   And hated going out to dance or dine;

Nor could he tolerate a single second,
   The social miseries that we incline
To call, good God! in their inane variety,
   The usages of elegant society.

XXVI.

Despite which, to the "drawing-room" he went,
   For beauty draws, we know, with single hairs,
(And paints with hares' feet, we might add, if bent
   On being cynical, authorial bears;
But as to be so is not our intent,
   Our muse to no such cruel length repairs,
But simply adds that our great hero's knock
Was heard in Clarges Street at twelve o'clock).

XXVII.

Beauty was ready, in a low-necked dress,
   That showed more shoulder, certainly, than sense;
And dragged behind a train in all the mess,
   That might have served, at just the same expense,
To cover up a bust which, we confess,
   Was fair to see, but might p'rhaps give offence
To leaner sisters and to envious tongues—
Not to forget the danger to her lungs.

XXVIII.

Beauty's mamma, a Countess of four-score,
   Showed even more of charms, though they were bony;
And with a dress, than Beauty's even lower,
   Displayed much skin, the hue of macaroni;
Whilst in a wig most palpable, she wore
   Three ostrich plumes,— poor Duan gave a groan, he
Felt tempted sore to get up an eruption
'Gainst going to Court with such bedecked corruption.

XXIX.

What sight on God's earth can be more disgusting
   Than painted, powder'd, and made-up old age?
Its scragginess on the beholder thrusting,
   And fighting time with feeble, wrinkled rage;
Covering with tinsel what has long been rusting,
   And writing hideous lies upon life's page.
Ruins, when left alone, are often grand,
But worthless when they show the plasterer's hand.

XXX.

But there's no time to moralise like this,—
   The carriage of the Countess waits below,
And offering his arm to ma' and miss,
   Our hero hands them in, and off they go

To plunge into the yaw-yawning abyss,
 And mingle with the never-ceasing flow
That fills the Mall and Bird-cage Walk, intent
 To crowd and take the Social Sacrament.

XXXI.

Full soon the bloated coachman had to stop
 His horses, as the carriage falls in line ;
And from the curious crowd begin to drop
 Remarks that made Jon Duan much incline
Out of the door of the barouche to pop,
 And visit them with punishment condign ;
Though all they said to put him in a passion
Was, " I say, here's an old ewe dressed lamb-fashion ! "

XXXII.

A tedious hour went by : the carriage crawled
 By slow degrees, and made its way by inches ;
The people chaff'd and cheer'd ; the p'licemen bawled,
 But not a high-born dame or maid that flinches.
Nor would they, one of them, have been appall'd
 Had all of Purgatory's pains and pinches
To be passed through to gain St. James's portal,
And courtesy low before a royal mortal !

XXXIII.

At last the gate is gained where sentries stand,
 Nor aim the inroad of the great to stay,
But grimly watch the fairest of the land
 As they pass in to mix in the wild fray ;
To join the seething, surging, swaying band
 That pushes on, its best respects to pay
To her, who for a whim—it can't be malice—
Will use what our Jeames calls St. James's "Palice."

XXXIV.

And then and there was hurrying to and fro,
 And hustling crowds, and symptoms of distress ;
And cheeks all pale, which but an hour ago
 Blush'd at the sight of their own loveliness ;
And there were sudden rents and sounds of woe,
 As skirts were torn and trampled in the press ;
Till Beauty, who that day was first presented,
Thought all "Who's Who" were certainly demented.

XXXV.

She clung to Duan's arm, and there was need,
 For like a wave the well-dressed mob surged on,
Went pouring forward with impetuous speed,
 Till she had been o'erwhelmed but for our Jon.

As 'twas, a rowel made her ankle bleed,
 And scores of feet her long train trod upon,
Till, well-nigh fainting, and with terror dumb,
She almost wished that she had never come.

XXXVI.

Beauty's mamma, a tried old dowager,
 Made better progress, worked her skinny arms
In neighbouring sides, till they made way for her,
 And op'ed a passage for her bony charms ;
She'd often pass'd the ordeal ; so the stir
 Filled her old crusty breast with no alarms :
Indeed, she must have been devoid of feeling,
As though her frame had undergone annealing.

XXXVII.

Thus on they struggled, inch by inch, and stair
 By stair ; now losing, now a little gaining ;
As though it were a life and death affair—
 As though the goal to which they all were straining
Were worth an endless lot of wear and tear,
 And efforts manifold, and arduous training—
As though, indeed, this courtly presentation
Worked out their future and their full salvation.

XXXVIII.

Still, 'tis no secret what they went to see,
 A widow'd lady ; getting near three-score ;
Still mourning, in a costume " cap"-à-pie,
 One dead some thirteen years ago and more ;
An estimable lady as may be,
 Yet looking on the whole thing as a bore.
Can we, if we dispassionately handle
The subject, say the game is worth the candle ?

XXXIX.

Duan thought not. If you the crown respect,
 Go to the Tower and see the whole regalia,
It costs but sixpence ; or if you affect
 The royal person, 'midst the penetralia
Of Tussaud's wax-works you may soon detect
 The waxen effigy ; and slobber daily a
Kiss or two upon the figure's garments,
To show you are not democratic "varmints."

XL.

But as to putting on absurd attire,
 And running risks of damage and mishap,
Exposing corns and clothes to danger dire
 To see a woman in a widow's cap—

George IV. As portrayed by the Tories.

"Who's your fat friend?"—*Beau Brummel*.
(*From the Originals, published by Hone.*)

Jon did not to such ecstasy aspire ;
　In point of fact, he did not care a rap—
'Spite all the gushing of the penny journals—
　To gaze at royalty *sans* its externals :

XLI.

But thousands do and thousands did that day,
　Whose history, so far, has been related :
And as these rhymes must not go on for aye,
　We think that Beauty long enough has waited
Upon the stairs ; we'll take her from the fray,
　And, with her pleasure all but dissipated,
We'll pass her on, as Yankees put it, slickly,
And bring her to the presence-chamber quickly.

XLII.

Stay ! for thy tread is where a sovereign sits !
　An Empire's Queen is seated on that chair !
Nor let a palsy overwhelm thy wits,
　When thou perceiv'st she is not lonely there ;—
Nor sink into the earth ; since fate permits
　Thine eyes to rest—if thou the sight canst bear—
On Princes and Princesses, fecund found,
In Guelphic lavishness arranged around.

XLIII.

See ! there is Albor's eldest,—language fails
　To write the reverence his face inspires :
The sight of Coming K—— our colour pales,
　Till loyalty lights up our facial fires.
God bless, by all means, Albert Prince of Wales !
　For certainly His blessing he requires.
Though happily we long ago have sunk all
Fear that he'll turn out like his gross great-uncle.

XLIV.

We do not mean the Duke of York, that cheat
　Who, saving that of nature, paid no debts;
Nor Sussex, that nonentity complete,
　Whose failings, fortunately, one forgets ;
Nor mean we Clarence, that buffoon effete
　Whose reign each loyal Englishman regrets—
Rascal or madman, it is hard to class him :
See for yourselves in "Greville's Memoirs" *passim*.

XLV.

We mean that other brother foul and false,
　That vulgar ruffian* whom no oath restrained ;
That bloated sot, who when too fat to valse,
　Was fit for nothing; that coarse king who's gained

* *Daily News*, Oct. 31, 1874.

More obloquy from history's assaults
Than any monarch who has o'er us reigned.
We would not visit harshly mere frivolity,
But where in George was one redeeming quality?

XLVI.

He lied; he swore; he was obscene and lewd;
And rakish past e'en what's a regal latitude;
He broke his word; his duties he eschew'd;
He understood not what was meant by gratitude;
The two great aims in life that he pursued
Were how to dress and how to strike an attitude—
Another king so mean and vile as he,
And England's kingly race would cease to be.

XLVII.

He was an utter brute, a sceptred thing,
A vampire sucking out his country's life;
Eclectic in his vice, a compound king,
Charles to his people, Henry to his wife.
Better by far that time again should bring
A Henry, or a Charles, and plunge in strife
Our country, than that it should e'er disgorge
Another heartless, soulless wretch like George.

XLVIII.

Our Heir-apparent will not be like this—
He mayn't be brilliant, but he is not brutal;
He may be simple, but it's not amiss
If that is all he is: he will not suit all
Tastes and desires, but it is well, we wis—
Though our opinion here may meet refutal—
Since kings are now for us but gilded toys,
To have one who won't make a fuss and noise.

XLIX.

Thank God! the eldest son's not like his sire,
A meddling, mean, and over-rated man;
A Bailiff on the throne we don't require,
However neatly he may scheme and plan
To make a property's return grow higher.
We can't forget the way Albor began
His steward's work; with what a screwy touch he
Wrung increased revenue from Cornwall's duchy.

L.

No one can say that our A. E. is stingy—
Indeed, his failing lies the other way;
Yet, though he on his capital infringe, he
Spends his money in a British way.

The coming Court will not be quite so dingy
As that o'er which his royal mamma has sway.
And though our notion may be very shocking,
We don't like sovereigns who "make a stocking."

LI.

Nor love we princes who have not large hearts—
Nor love we much the Duke of Edinburgh;
He lives too late. A young man of his parts
Would well have represented a "close" borough.
As 'tis, no thought incongruous ever starts
At finding him a Scotchmen's duke, for thorough
Is the connection 'twixt them, though 'tis troubling
To find that he's not dubbed the Duke of Doubling.

LII.

A sailor should be generous and hearty;
An English prince 'fore all should not be mean;
And whilst rememb'ring statements made *ex parte*
Must not be credited too much, we glean
That modern Athens' duke, however smart he
Upon the fiddle plays, yet has not been
So wise as to despise all petty things,
And keep his scrapings for his fiddle-strings.

LIII.

We had a hope, being married, he'd improve—
He had a lot of money with his Mary,—
We'll wish some generous impulses will move
Our new Princess, and that, like some good fairy,
She'll lift her Alfred from his stingy groove,
And make him for the future very chary
Of any acts like those of him recorded,
Which are, to put it mildly, mean and sordid.

LIV.

It gives our enemies so good a handle
To chaff our institutions and our crown,
When princes make themselves a peg for scandal,
And furnish tittle-tattle for the town.
For they should clearly learn to firm withstand all
Fishy transactions sliming their renown;
And those who're near the Princess should advise
  her
On no account let Alfred be a miser.

LV.

Nor let him show the instincts of a trader;
Nor bargain with his friends in search of gain;
But, that his actions never may degrade her,
Let him from City ways henceforth refrain.

JON DUAN.

His star is now most surely in its nadir,
  But there is time the zenith to regain;
Then we will let the Malta business * slip,
  And not remember his Australian trip.

LVI.

And whilst addressing Marie, we may add
  We hope it is not true she made a fuss,
And summoned to her aid her royal dad,
  Because a princess who's most dear to us
Declined to listen to her foolish fad,
  Or questions of precedence to discuss.
But if 'tis true, then Marie must take care
Lest she is called the little Russian Bear.

LVII.

Our coming Monarch's Consort's loved most dearly,
  Loyal respect for her is most emphatic;
And whosoever her attacks, is clearly
  By no means well-advised or diplomatic;
We'll trust that Marie knew no better, merely
  Having been bred in Russ ways autocratic.
Yet, for the future, if she'd keep her place,
She mustn't show the Tartar, but learn grace.

LVIII.

But all this time the royal party waits—
  Louise and Arthur, Uncle George and Lorne;
And pretty 'Trixy, who, if rumour states
  The truth, will soon be to the altar borne.
See Christian, too, who doubtless stands and rates
  His luck, that from his Fatherland he's torn.
Poor fellow! notice his dejected carriage—
He's thinking of his morganatic marriage.

Thumb-Nail Sketches from The Academy.

LIX.

He's thinking of the *frau* he left behind him,
  Of sauer-kraut perchance, and Lager beer;
And wondering that the skein the Parcæ wind him
  Has guided him so comfortably here;
With such a kind mamma-in-law to find him
  In pocket-money, and with lots a year
As ranger of an English park.—'Tis strange
How those dear Germans like our parks to range.†

---

* As boys say—Ask the "Governor" to tell you the story.

† "I will be thy park, and thou shalt be my deer."—
Shakspeare's *Venus and Adonis*.

LX.

At home they starve, but here they live in clover;
  Our best positions are at their command:
Since Coburg-Gotha's prince to us came over,
  Legions of Deutchland's princelings seek our land;
And Queenly eyes and ears swiftly discover
  The hidden virtues of that German band.
But though we've had experience of dozens,
There's not much love lost for these German-
  "cozens."

LXI.

A look of anger spreads o'er Kamdux' face,
  As though the *Siliad* he just had read.
The officer would be in sorry case
  Who now approached our army's titled head;
For Uncle George does not belie his race,
  But swears and blusters—so the *Siliad* said—
As though he had been one of those commanders
Who fought years since with Corporal Trim in
  Flanders.

LXII.

His mind is very likely burdened now
  With doubts about his army's straps and buckles;
And care is seated on his massive brow,
  Because he fears how military "suckles"
Will to his next new button-edict bow;
  Whilst many a line his Guelphic features puckles
As he decides he will, in any case,
Curtail the width of sergeant-majors' lace.

LXIII.

And here our muse breaks off to sing All hail,
  Great army tailor! and hail! Prince Commander,
Thou burker of reforms, that needs must fail
  Whilst statesmen to the Georgic wishes pander;
Thou duke of details! 'tis of no avail,
  Except for rhyme, to call thee Alexander:—
For when thou sittest down to weep and falter,
Tis 'cause thou'st no more uniforms to alter.

LXIV.

Now, look at poor young Lorne—his face averring
  That, though a royal princess he has got,
He's neither fish, nor joint, nor good red-herring,
  Thanks to the special nature of his lot;
Snubbed by the Court: the world beneath inferring
  He's now no part in it—he p'rhaps is not
So happy as he might be, and may rue
He ever played so very high for "Loo."

LXV.

Too long our blushing Beauty's been neglected,
  It's now her turn to figure on the scene.
For months a mistress has her steps directed,
  That she herself may properly demean,
May backwards walk, and bow low, as expected
  When subjects dare to pass before their Queen.
All natural instincts have to be dispersed,
When that play called "Society" 's rehearsed.

LXVI.

Society! O what a hideous sham
  Is veiled and masked beneath that specious name!
Society! its mission is to damn,
  To curse, and blight; to burn with withering flame
All that is worthiest in us—to cram
  The world with polished hypocrites, who claim
To sin, of right—Society has said it—
And think their crimes are greatly to their credit!

LXVII.

What worships rank, and makes a god of gold?
  What turns fair women into painted frights?
What tempts to vice and villainy untold?
  And claims from all of us its devilish rites?
What prompts ambition, base and uncontrolled?
  What never on the side of mercy fights?
What causes sin in horrible variety?—
Mostly, the demon that we call Society.

LXVIII.

'Tis in obedience to its unwrit laws
  We bow beneath the iron yoke of Fashion;
In its stern edicts see the primal cause
  Why we as sin treat every healthy passion—
Why we a daughter sell, without a pause,
  As though she were a Georgian or Circassian—
Yet shudder when we meet a painted harlot,
And say, "Thank God!" that she is not our
  Charlotte.

LXIX.

And what is Charlotte, then, in Heaven's name?
  She did not love the fellow that she married;
But he some hundred thousand pounds could claim,
  And such a weapon could not well be parried.*

---

* Although, be it observed, the weapon in question was undoubtedly "blunt."

She sold herself for life.—Is't not the same
  As though the sale but brief possession carried?
We think it worse—though Mother Church has
    prayed
The sordid union may be fruitful made.

LXX.

And yet Society makes much of Charlotte,
  And takes her to its bosom with delight,
Receives effusively the life-long harlot—
  But curses her who sins but for a night,
Expels her from its midst—her sins are scarlet,
  And ne'er can be atoned for in its sight.
Thus serves two ends—the Social Evil nourishing,
And keeping the Divorce Court cause-list flourish-
    ing.

LXXI.

But it is vain of us to run a-tilt
  Against Society with bitter verses,
Its fabric is by far too firmly built
  To yield to them; it only yields to purses.
We will not longer linger on its guilt,
  Save to bestow upon it final curses,
And in the name of all that's pure and holy,
Denounce it and its sinful doings wholly!

LXXII.

In Beauty's name denounce it;—though but twenty,
  She'd learn'd some of its lessons from her mother;
And how her appetite to check and smother;
She'd learned to lace too tight—to use a plenty
  Of toilet adjuncts: rouge, and many another
Such weighty preparation.—*Gott in Himmel!*
He's much to answer for, has Monsieur Rimmel.

LXXIII.

She'd learn'd to flirt, and calmly to cast off
  The man she'd loved, when he his money lost;
She had a lisp and an affected cough,
  And valued things according to their cost.
She'd practised, too, the usual sneer and scoff,
  And could not bear her slightest wishes cross'd;
In fact, although out of her teens but lately,
She had advanced in worldly knowledge greatly.

LXXIV.

Still, as we've said, 'twas her first drawing-room.
  She'd been in mobs before at "drums" and dances,
But ne'er before this had it been her doom
  To mix in such a mob as that which chances

When Queen Victoria comes forth from her gloom,
   And, following out one of her widowed fancies,
Won't hold receptions where there's space to spare,
But at St. James's has a crush and scare.

LXXV.

'Twas well she had Jon Duan at her side
   To whisper in her ear and make her brave;
"Now, go!" he said, when Beauty's name was cried;
   And Beauty did go then, and by a shave
Just managed not to fall down, as she tried
   To show the Queen she knew how to behave,
By walking backwards, when she'd courtesied low,
And had out at a distant door to go.

LXXVI.

Court etiquette of course must be maintained;
   But, in the name of common sense and reason,
This "backwards" business long enough has reigned;
   Such fooleries have long since had their season.
If subjects from such crab-like steps refrained,
   Lèse-majeste, wouldst call it, or high treason?
Surely one can the Sovereign love and honour,
Although his back were sometimes turned upon her.

LXXVII.

Poor Beauty had a very near escape,
   For, as she from the presence retrograded,
A gouty General interposed his shape;
   And had not watchful Duan once more aided,
His charge had fell into a pretty scrape.
   As 'twas, the warrior's steel her train invaded,
And, making in it quite a deep incision,
Writ 'mongst its folds much long and short division.

LXXVIII.

Still she escaped uninjured save in dress,
   And that was cause for some congratulation;
Though at that stage 'twas early to express
   A sense of gratitude or exultation;
For there was yet to come, we must confess,
   The worst alarm, the greatest consternation.
To get in was a "caution;" *sans* a doubt,
'Twas twenty times more trouble to get out!

LXXIX.

It was but quitting frying-pan for fire,
   'Twas very "hot," poor Beauty quickly found;
The crowd was worse; the temperature was higher;
   And there were swords that hitched, and heels that ground;—
Patrician faces glared with anger dire,
   Patricians strove like porkers in a pound;
And many plainly muttered observations
Sounded extremely like to execrations.

LXXX.

Two hours they pushed and pressed from pen to pen,
   And there was nothing there to drink or eat;
A biscuit and a glass of wine would, then,
   Have fetched a price we scarcely dare repeat,—
For tender girls were faint; and lusty men
   For very hunger scarce could keep their feet.
Meantime, the Sovereign serenely rests
Upon her chair, nor troubles 'bout her guests.

LXXXI.

Thus Duan thought:—"'Tis inconsiderate, very;
   Either hold drawing-rooms where there is space,
Or give the weary guests a glass of sherry,
   When they've to struggle so from place to place;
The cost would not be so extraordinary—
   The boon would priceless be in many a case;
For it is apt both strong and weak to 'flummox,'
To push for several hours on empty stomachs!"

LXXXII.

Beauty, for instance, had no breakfast eaten,
   Excitement took away her appetite;—
By one o'clock she felt she was dead-beaten:
   But there was not a chance of sup or bite.
At four, resignedly, she took her seat on
   A chair our hero found, and fainted quite;
And then for twenty minutes she'd to stay
Before her mother's carriage stopped the way.

LXXXIII.

And what a scene she left!—of fainting girls,
   And gasping duchesses, and sinking dames;
Confusion everywhere the people whirls,
   'Midst hasty shouts and calling out of names;

And all the ground is strewn with scraps and curls,
  And shreds of stuff and beads which no one claims,
Whilst England's highest-born, with might and main,
Fight like a gallery crowd at Drury Lane.

LXXXIV.

The morn beheld them full of lusty life,
  In radiant toilets decked and proudly gay :
Four hours of pushing toil and crushing strife,
  And who so tattered and so limp as they?
Now rents are everywhere and rags are rife—
  Destruction has succeeded to display ;
And wondrous costumes, "built" by foreign artistes,
Are wreck'd and ruined like the Bonapartists !

LXXXV.

Sweet Mistress, why let such a scandal be,
  When thy fond subjects flock to see thy face ?
Thou wilt now to its reformation see,
  And act as doth become thy royal race ;
For all that read this will with us agree,
  That such a state of things is a disgrace.
And if your Majesty won't trust our rhymes,
We just refer you to last July's "*Times*."

LXXXVI.

That night, when Beauty had devoured her dinner,
  And her mamma had filled up all her creases—
For, truth to tell, that very ancient sinner
  Had almost literally been pulled to pieces—
Jon Duan, looking p'rhaps a little thinner,
  Sits down, when casual conversation ceases,
At the piano, and with anger rising,
Performed the following piece of improvising.

The Rout of Belgravia.

I.

The Belgravians came down on the Queen in her hold,
And their costumes were gleaming with purple and gold,
And the sheen of their jewels was like stars on the sea,
As their chariots roll'd proudly down Piccadill-ee.

2.

Like the leaves of *Le Follet* when summer is green,
That host in its glory at noontide was seen;
Like the leaves of a toy-book all thumb-marked and worn,
That host four hours later was tattered and torn.

3.

For the crush of the crowd, which was eager and vast,
Had rumpled and ruin'd and wreck'd as it pass'd;
And the eyes of the wearer wax'd angry in haste,
As gathers just sewn were dragged out at the waist.

4.

And there lay the feather and fan, side by side,
But no longer they nodded or waved in their pride;
And there lay lace flounces, and ruching in slips,
And spur-torn material in plentiful strips.

5.

And there were odd gauntlets, and pieces of hair;
And fragments of back-combs, and slippers were there;

And the gay were all silent; their mirth was all hush'd;
Whilst the dew-drops stood out on the brows of the crush'd.

6.

And the dames of Belgravia were loud in their wail,
And the matrons of Mayfair all took up the tale;
And they vow, as they hurry, unnerved, from the scene,
That it's no trifling matter to call on the Queen.

LXXXVII.

Soon after, seeing Beauty was so weary,
  Jon Duan press'd her hand and said "Goodbye!"
And, fancying that his room would be too dreary,
  He bade a hansom to far Fulham hie.
Why he should go down there we leave a query,
  Lest some who read these lines should say "Fie! fie!"
Though from this hint we cannot well refrain,
That p'rhaps he wished to go to "court" again.

---

[1] The well-known exclamation of the Spanish Ambassador to Elizabeth's Court—"I have seen the head of the English Church dancing!"—may be remembered. To his notion there was something strikingly incongruous in the grave and lawful governess of the Church stepping it merrily with the favourite gentlemen of the Court. What would that Spanish Ambassador have exclaimed had he witnessed the scene detailed in the next note? What should we think now of Elizabeth if she had danced with a stable-help?

[2] Her Majesty gave a ball at Balmoral, on Friday. In the course of the evening Her Majesty danced for the first time since the death of the Prince Consort. She danced with Prince Albert Victor and Prince George, sons of the Prince of Wales, and afterwards took part in a reel with John Brown, her attendant, and Donald Stewart, gamekeeper.—*The Leeds Weekly News*, Saturday, June 6th, 1874.

THUMB-NAIL SKETCHES FROM THE ACADEMY.

Canto The Third.

I.

THERE stands, or once stood, for on several pleas,
   It's most unsafe to use the present tense
In speaking of these paper argosies
   That pirate daily all a lounger's pence;
And have to labour against heavy seas,
   And sail, most of them, in a fog as dense
As any that rasps London lungs quite raw—
Then, go to pieces on the rocks of law:

II.

So there stood once—we'll say once on a time—
   A time when newspapers were not a "spec,"
Consisting in the offering for a dime
   Of seven murders, one rape, ditto wreck,
Critiques on the Academy, sublime,
   The last accouchement of the Princess Teck,
Fashionable scandals, exits and arrivals—
All latest news—picked from the morning rivals—

III.

There stood, then, but a few doors from the Strand,
   A dingy mansion, such as is best fitted
To shrine that fourth estate, which rules the land—
   That is to say, outrageously pock-pitted
And tumble-down, with proofs of devil's hand
   On every door, with windows grimed and gritted,
And so clothed in old broad-sheets that it stood
For almanack to all the neighbourhood.

IV.

The reader has a character to lose—
   Or one to sell; and characters are cheap
In offices of newspapers that choose
   To rather scandalise than let one sleep;
And therefore all concerning them is news;
   And being curious, you long to peep
At places where they scarify Disraeli,
Or tell Lord Salisbury his conduct's scaly.

V.

A crowd of ragamuffins in a court,
   Who wait for papers, playing pitch and toss;
Cabmen and loafers ready at retort,
   And generally talking of a "'oss";

A dribbling stream who "flimsily" report,
  And feel Sir Roger a tremendous loss ;
Surely a peeler—sometimes an M.P. ;
This is the usual *mise en scène* you see.

VI.

Within the temple, order of the sternest
  Prevails, supported by a well-drilled staff.
Woe to thee, compos., if a pipe thou burnest !
Woe to thee, reader, if thou dar'st to laugh !
Here everybody must appear in earnest ;
  They're all half theologians here, and half
Teetotallers ; their aim is strict propriety—
They're read in families of Quivering piety.

VII.

Respectability, you Juggernaut,
  You fetish insular and insolent,
You're everywhere ! the nation's neck you've caught
  In one big noose—a white cravat ; you've sent
Pecksniff to Parliament, and 'gainst us wrought
  The worst of ills—on humbugs ever bent ;
But never did we deem you so infernal
As when you set up your own ha'penny journal.

VIII.

There are so many Mrs. Grundys preaching
  A blind obedience to your nods and firmans ;
There are so many Mr. Podsnaps teaching
  Your gospel to the French and Turks and Germans—
Who're all Bohemian vagrants and want breeching—
  The stage and pulpit echo with your sermons—
A thing they never did for Dr. Paley—
Surely you're not obliged to print them daily !

IX.

But we must bow, for we must read ;—a want
  That makes us more dyspeptic than our sires,
And also favours an increase of cant ;
  For though to highest thought a man aspires,
He can't be always reading Hume and Kant,
  Nor Swinburne, nor the rest of the high-flyers.
The fire divine fatigues—one takes to tapers,
That is to say, one reads the daily papers.

X.

The sheet in question, then, is widely read,
  Chiefly by cabmen—and it's not elating,
For when they've got that pure prose in their head,
  They always sixpence ask, at least, for waiting.
Its politics are liberal, too, 'tis said,
  Which means they're radical with silver plating ;
But all sorts write in it, Rad, Whig, or Tory,
With any coloured ink, buff, blue, or gory.

XI.

Mong writers, printers, clerks, and advertisers,
  All in a hurry and as grave as Job,
Moved by a noble rage to print the Kaiser's
  Last ukase half an hour before the *Globe*—
For that's true journalism, though paid disguisers
  Essay with pompous phrase the truth to robe ;—
Among these, then, Jon Duan passed ; his pocket
Bulged with MSS. 'twould take an hour to docket.

XII.

He went towards the pigeon-hole to which
  The needle's eye of Scripture is a fool—
That's a mere figure to rebuke the rich—
  Here poor and wealthy find their welcome cool ;—
Why, Saint Augustine might step from his niche,
  And knock, and they'd not offer him a stool,
Unless he'd cry " No Popery," or would make
A speech or two supporting Miss Jex Blake.

XIII.

There was another way, and that Jon Duan
  By chance alone and innocently took.
One gets a civil letter written to one
  By some famed author of a Bill or book—
If it's a woman—she must be a blue 'un ;
  They'll print the missive forthwith, and will look
Thankfully on you ; one of their anxieties
Is to seem popular with notorieties.

XIV.

Up went Jon Duan's lucky name, and soon
  With beating heart and pulse his card he followed.
Downstairs the steam-press hummed its drowsy tune,
  Clerks passed in corridors, and urchins hollo'd ;
He heard naught, but walked on as in a swoon,
  Fancying some free and fearless presence hallowed

The creaking floors, the wall's perspiring dun
 blank—
Spirit of Wilkes, Swift, Junius, Jerrold, Fonblanque.

XV.

I see a smile come to the reader's eyes,
 Which view, of course, all things thro' microscopes,
And read between the lines of leaders—lies;
 The reader, naturally, "knows the ropes"
In these press matters: we apologise;
 But faith, our hero's sadly young, and hopes
Love's not all lust nor Liberty an ogress—
 And thinks—the simpleton—the press means progress.

XVI.

Forgive him. You may hear how he was punished;
 How soon the warm, quick blood oozed cooler, calmer;
How women laughed at him, and men admonished;
 How he grew deaf unto the illusive charmer,—
Was never grieved, delighted, nor astonished,
 Dined, slept, walked, flirted in a suit of armour—
In short, so perfect got, you scarce could hit on
 A prettier portrait of the ideal Briton.

XVII.

But now we have left him innocent and blushing—
 Remembering those manuscripts, before
A door whereon, awe-struck, he read the crushing,
 August, and gorgeous title: Editor!
He cleared his throat, pulled down his cuffs, and pushing
 With timid touches that Plutonian door,
Which, opening promptly, swung back with a slam,—
 He saw the great chief—eating bread and jam!

XVIII.

Jon Duan brought a note from Castelar,
 One from Caprera, one from bold Bazaine;—
So he was well received. These heroes are
 Acquaintances of value, for they deign
Write numerous letters on the Carlist war,
 Peace Congresses, Courts Martial; and it's plain
Each one's a puff for which he thanks them deeply—
 Besides, they serve to fill the paper cheaply.

XIX.

After Jon Duan had been sagely pumped,
 Concerning all he'd seen in his excursions,
He mustered up some confidence, and plumped
 Into the theme of literary exertions.
He said: "I am, Sir, what you may call—stumped"—
 (The chief sighed at neologists' perversions)—
"I've loved, loafed, danced, drank, gambled, and played polo;
 I'd try at Journalism—tho' they say it's so low!

XX.

" I want to write—above all to be printed;
 The modern mania burns within my breast.
I've some experience, as I just now hinted,
 Perhaps 'twould give my articles a zest.
Would, now, this sonnet——" Here his listener squinted
 At a broadsheet a boy presented. "Pest!"
Exclaimed the Editor; "the sub's wits wander,
 Tell him to put in ' Latest from Santander!'"

XXI.

Then, blandly turning round: "You mentioned Verses!
 Young man, you're in a very vicious path.
They are among an Editor's chief curses.
 I have now—pray don't whisper it in Gath—
Three spinsters who have met with sore reverses,
 Ten Tuppers, seven Swinburnes, very wroth,
All writing daily and requesting answers
 Concerning all their madrigals and " stanzers."

XXII.

Of course, Jon Duan said he'd naught in common
 With humble rhymsters, who essay to climb
Parnassus in list slippers. He'd seen human
 Nature almost in every phase and clime;
And didn't sing the usual song of Woman
 In Alexandrines, elephants of rhyme;
He'd read a specimen—and really grew so
 Pressing, at last the bland chief bade him do so.

Mademoiselle Prudhomme.

Her dress is high, and there's nothing within.
 Polished in Clapham, its pale flowers' pick,
She is just twenty-one and spruce as a pin,—
 Her head is the only thing she has thick.

A meagre bosom, and shoulder, and mind,
   A meagre mouth, that will never miss
The tender touch it will never find—
   The passionate pulse of a lover's kiss.

The eyes speak no language, much less a soul;
   The brows are faint, and the forehead is spare,
And low and empty. Then over the whole
   That fool's straw crown of submissive hair.

O, happy the man with wrought-iron nerves,
   Who shall say of this tempting morsel, "Mine"—
O treasure in pottery and preserves—
   O Hebe, careful of gooseberry wine!

Has it a heart? oh, arise and appeal,
   Lost sisters, that famine and cold destroyed;
Will you prick to pity the hearts that feel
   For Magdalen less than Aurora Floyd?

Has it a mind? Come, arise and unfold,
   Redeemer, the lives to be raised at last!
Is there room for thought in the brains that hold
   Kitchen and nursery sufficiently vast?

And yet she shall be a woman in fine;
   Some one will worship her thimble and fan,
Some one grow drunk on her gooseberry wine;
   And she'll find a husband—perhaps a man.

For fate will be good and provide one—meek,
   And long, and good, and foolish, and flat,
A curate—immaculate, sour and sleek,
   A Pillar of Grace with a Blanched Cravat!

And duly the two will endow their kind
   With the old Clapham growth as spruce as a pin;
Meagre in bosom, and shoulder, and mind,
   Her horrible virtue sanctifies sin.

Mademoiselle Prudhomme will hamper and stay
   The world's march onwards—will gossip and dress,
And sew, and suckle, and dine, and pray:
   "Madonna Grundy have pity or bless;"—

Mademoiselle Prudhomme will simper and slay
   "Strong Minds," with her poor little anodyne wit; .
And flatter herself as she's dying one day,
   She's a heart—while the sawdust leaks out of it.

XXIII.

This was a little piece of lyric flattery;
   For anyone not quite a savage knows
Our Editor's renowned for milk and watery
   Elegies on the sweeter sex's woes.
He thought their masters too much given to battery
   With fire-irons, doubled fists, and hobnailed shoes,
Which don't, he said, reform domestic Tartars;—
   At home, 'tis said, *he* suffers for the martyrs.

XXIV.

He said Jon Duan's principles were proper;
   He liked the matter and he liked the name;
And then abruptly he applied a stopper
   To all the poet's rising hopes of fame.
"The fact is, such things are not worth a copper.
   Your young enthusiasm I don't blame;
But really you don't think—it is too funny!—
You don't think that this kind of thing's worth money!

XXV.

"No man writes poetry to-day, unless
   He's leisure, and some hundreds sure a year—
Ev'n then he'll often find that going to press,
   Mean's going to Queer Street, E.C.; and when there
He'll find the Registrar no whit the less
   Severe, because he's only paid too dear
For writing verse—and not for acting prose—
At St. John's Wood with Miss or Madame Chose.

XXVI.

"The Press, sir, is the modern channel flowing
   To Pactolus: compress into a column
Your finest thought, your dreams most grand and glowing;
   Frequent good clubs; grow staid, and stout, and solemn;
And, with a little cringing and kotowing,
   Your fortune's made. I don't want to extol 'em,
But we've a few bards of imagination—
They're now reporting a Great Conflagration.

XXVII.

"We may not want bays, laurels, crowns, and mitres;
   We'd do without some J.P.s and policemen;
We'd do without some lawyers and some fighters—
   The fools who bully, and the knaves who fleece men;

THUMB-NAIL SKETCHES FROM THE ACADEMY.

But, sir, this Age *must* have its ready writers—
  Not too profound, but aiming to release men,
  By aid of half a dozen library shelves,
  From that dread task of thinking for themselves."

XXVIII.

Humility, that worst of all good qualities—
  And Heaven knows there's plenty bad enough!—
Is common, but Jon Duan wouldn't call it his.
  He knew his intellect was of the stuff
That makes men feel above such vain frivolities;
  He rhymed, it's true; but he was also tough
In logic, versed in art, a studious reader,
So he sat down and wrote a social leader.

XXIX.

You know the social leader—it's designed
  To please the ladies o'er the morning toast.
We've written them ourselves sometimes, and find
  Wrecks, royal visits, and divorces, most
Apt to enthrall the lovely creatures' mind.
  A breach of promise isn't bad; you coast
Round naughty subjects, show an inch of stocking,
Observing all the while: How very shocking!

XXX.

We know the bits to quote to show your learning,
  And those to prove your feeling or your humour;
Swift, Hook, Hood, Smith, or Jerrold; the discerning
  Reader will add the rest; Pepys, Evelyn, Hume, or
Bacon, La Rochefoucauld—they all bear churning
  In frothy paragraphs; and one or two more
Make up a hodge-podge which, served after warming,
People not yet at Earlswood call quite charming.

XXXI.

I think Jon Duan tried his 'prentice hand
  At something more or less to do with Beer
(What hasn't in this free and thirsty land?),
  He lashed tremendously, he had no fear;
On highly moral grounds he took his stand,
  And vigorously, with biting jest and jeer,
Spoke out about the publicans' last grievance,
To be assuaged by brewers at St. Stephen's.

XXXII.

"Highly commendable," the chief observed;
  And mildly glowed the austere spectacles;
"From those great principles I've never swerved.
  But this will never do—our paper sells—

(Of course I know your strictures are deserved)—
  Largely in cafés, taverns, and hotels ;
We have sent out poor Truth dress'd so succinctly,
  She's caught cold—that's why she don't speak distinctly."

XXXIII.

Jon Duan, downcast and confused was standing,
  Thinking he'd ne'er a leader read again,
His mind with notions new and strange expanding ;
  When some one cried : " Put in my news from Spain."
And bounding upstairs, bumped him on the landing,
  A stranger, who's—we may as well explain,
Mr. Maloy, a " special," who makes free
To date from Irun, write in Bloomsbury.

XXXIV.

There's nothing like this odd kind of collision—
  If one's not seeking rhymes or lost one's purse—
As introduction, it makes an incision
  Into that Saxon cloak of pride we curse
But still will wear, through death, despair, division,
  The Robe of Nessus, of Ovidian verse—
At least to-day it made Jon Duan enter
A friendship in which he soon found a Mentor.

XXXV.

Fleet Street, receive the writers' salutation!
  We never pass through tottering Temple Bar,
Without a feeling of profound elation
  At the grand panorama stretched afar ;
We take our hats off, and from Ludgate Station
  See Genius coming, in triumphal car,
And with a flaming crest, and waving pinions,
Beating the boundaries of its own dominions.

XXXVI.

We see the nation's brain, its best lobe seething
  In the strong throb and clamour of the road :
We see the legion of the teachers sheathing
  Their pens in monkish creed, and Pecksniff's code;
'Tis here each high idea begins its breathing,
  From here it takes its armèd flight abroad—
To fall, a thunderbolt on thrones and steeples—
To fall, as manna, to the calling peoples.

XXXVII.

Temple of Fame, all stained with dust and grime,
  In air oft foul, in architecture heavy,
We freedom see and knowledge guard, sublime,
  Thy low dark eaves ; and in thy courts a bevy
Of muses, singing some old London rhyme ;
  And then—and then we see the tribe of Levy
Entering their broughams with smug ostentation—
And, somehow, that arrests our inspiration.

XXXVIII.

We drop back to the rôle of chronicler,
  Following Jon Duan and his new-found friend,
Maloy. That juvenile philosopher
  Descanted freely on the aim and end
Of literature ; and glibly could refer
  To several famous gentlemen who've penned
Verse, novels, essays, which we've all admired—
Not knowing how the authors were inspired.

XXXIX.

Maloy was made to be an interviewer,
  There was no Fleet Street curtain and no blind
He didn't raise, and with some comments truer
  Than tender, scarify the scribes behind.
Here rose a hiccough, there a hallelujah—
  Not far from Shoe Lane once the two combined—
Here they declare the Ballot Act's a sad law—
Here kid-glove Radicals haw-haw at Bradlaugh.

XL.

Here, to the left, two-pennyworth of gall
  Wars with two-pennyworth of gall and water,
One shrieking " Yankee !" and the other " Gaul!"
  And threatening weekly libel suits and slaughter.
Here lies poor Punch, a Taylor sews his pall,
  While opposite there stands the brick and mortar
Palace of Truth, where, to instruct us, Stanley
Finds out the Nile, while Greenwood hunts at Hanley.

XLI.

Here's the great factory where they puff the Premier,
  The Lords, the Bishops, Publicans and Princes
Only they'd make the soft-soap rather creamier,
  Were it not that my Lord of Salisbury winces ;
Besides tow'rds a new rival, rather dreamier,
  Favour at times the Government evinces.
They sell though, still, from poppies of their growing,
The largest pennyworth of opium going.

XLII.

The best of chatterers is a scandal-monger ;
  His pills are bitter, and he gilds a bit ;
And all men, though they smirk and say No, hunger
  To have their famous neighbours' weazands slit.

So laughed Jon Duan as Maloy grew stronger
In aphorisms—those stalactites of wit;
And when they had dined *en garçon* at the
"Mitre,"
Resolved he'd die, or be a well-known writer.

XLIII.

A writer—bravo! The idea's not new,
At least, it's shared by all the Civil Service;
The Bar, the Church, and in the Army, too,
It rages with the force of several scurvies;
But, faith, the aim, with this unique reserve, is
As good as any British youths pursue—
It's mostly, when a lad is fresh from school
A horse, champagne, Anonyma, or pool.

XLIV.

"But what's your special genius, talent, line—
Prose, verse, or 'rhythmic Saxon,' like dear Dixon?
Wish you to scandalise, or mildly shine?
Swinburne's or Houghton's, which renown d'you
fix on?
Come, choose your mate among the tuneful Nine;
There's Tupper's Twaddle, and Buchanan's
Vixen;
That Pale One, made O'Shaughnessy's by mar-
riage—
And Browning's Blue, oft subject to miscarriage.

XLV.

"There's Bret Harte's Yankee—though she does
say d——n,
She's quite the lady in her principles.
And what d'you say to Lockyer's, a *grande dame*
Coiffée at moments *à la* cap and bells?
There's Tennyson's would serve you like a lamb,
And teach you to 'ring out wild bells,' and knells,
Whene'er a German, corpulent and moral,
Expires, lies in, or marries, at Balmoral.

XLVI.

"But maybe odder fancies make you moody—
Perhaps you'd write your novel, like your neigh-
bours;
Walk up—make your selection: There's the goody,
The gamy, the idyllic; arduous labours
Which bring in millions—unto Mr. Mudie:
The military, full of oaths and sabres,
The hectic, allegoric, or the pastoral—
But only Jeaffreson has time to master all.

XLVII.

"The eight vols. like George Eliot's—there's a field
Fresh, wide, and rich in fine food for the flail;
But pray wear spectacles ; it doesn't yield
 Unless you analyse each slug and snail ;
And read theology in blocks congealed
 From safes of Kant, Spinoza, Reid, and Bayle ;
Unless, too, you've a friend, and can wade through his
 Complete Edition of the Works of Lewes.

XLVIII.

"I might suggest likewise those smaller spheres
 Where several virgins, widows—even wives—
But husbands hinder terribly, one hears—
 Are writing novels for their very lives.
Oh, if they'd do it in their uglier years—
 Ink's a cosmetic when old age arrives ;
But no, the dears have scarce left pinafores,
Before they're knocking at Sam Tinsley's doors.

XLIX.

"And what astounding manuscripts they carry,
 These innocents just fresh from Mangnall's Questions!
How very oddly all their heroines marry !
 How very frequently the very best shuns
Her Lord and Master, for Tom, and Dick, and Harry—
 Who're always in the Guards, have good digestions,
Tawny moustaches, 'lean flanks'—charming Satans,
Come up from Hell in kid gloves and mail phaetons.

L.

"Pardon, Miss Muloch and Miss Yonge—you're free
 From any taint the moralist impure rates ;—
O, that your world were real, that we might be
 All Lady Bountifuls and model curates,
Talking good grammar o'er eternal tea,
 With one ambition—to reduce the poor rates !
But fie ! Miss Braddon, Broughton, Ouida—you
Seduce us from the Band of Hope Review.

LI.

"Reade, Lawrance, Yates, and Holme Lee, Kingsley, Grant,
 Black the idyllic, Collins (Mortimer),
Collins, called Wilkie, Trollope, whom they vaunt
 In proud Belgravia, and in Westminster;
Grave Farjeon, and E. Jenkins, who decant
 The wine of Dickens in a cullender ;
And then there's—but how dare you keep your hat on ?—
That proud provincial Editor, Joe Hatton !

LII.

"'J'en passe et des meilleurs,'" Maloy concluded :
 "Fitzgerald, Oliphant, George Meredith,
Sell ; so perhaps they shouldn't be excluded ;
 Whyte Melville, Francillon, are men of pith ;
I also might have said that one or two did
 Wonders to neutralize the brand of Smith ;—
But catalogues were ever an infliction—
E'en Homer's ships—far lighter than some fiction.

LIII.

"One's born a woman ; one becomes a man.
 Jon Duan, when you write, bear this in mind,
And interest the ladies if you can;
 For all the wide world over, womankind
Loves the same books ; male readers pry and scan ;
 Boys, young men, fogies, different authors find—
But schoolgirl, grandmamma, French, German, Briton—
Show me the woman who don't dote on Lytton.

LIV.

"But he's their classic. You, the modern, must
 Select your heroes and your heroines
From their own drawing-rooms, and then adjust
 Your dolls in patchworks made of all the sins ;
Be roué, and disclose a bit of bust,
 Raise Dolly Vardens o'er some shapely shins ;
Suggest, but don't be crude ; and don't say Vice—
But hint your villain's conduct isn't nice.

LV.

"And then, slang, croquet, champagne, clubs, and horses ;
 Plump painted 'persons,' who will bear the blame
For all misguided heroes' evil courses;
 Bad French, when sloven English is too tame ;
Danseuses and Guardsmen, Duchesses, divorces—
 Mix up and spice—the elixir this, of fame
Of modern Balzacs—of this pure and mighty
Age, that's produced *two* publishers for 'Clytie.'"

LVI.

Here poor Jon Duan rose and paid the bill.
  "But you must choose your set as well as style,"
Pursued Maloy, who, though not meaning ill,
  Was apt to make his inch of talk a mile.
"There is a spectacle hard by that will
  Make plain my meaning in a little while."
A few steps brought them to a—well, a "pub"—
(Rhyme's a great leveller), and a liter'ry club.

LVII.

It is the Great Club of the Disappointed
  And bald Bohemian mediocrities,
Who think the century is all disjointed,
  Because they can't direct it as they please;
And so they choose to make their own Anointed,
  Regardless of the outer world's decrees;
No matter how their idols it excoriates,
Here they're all statesmen, M.P.s, R.A.s, Laureates.

LVIII.

There's Hack, their novelist; George Eliot quakes
  When one of his Scotch pastorals appears;
And Mr. Browning, too, 'tis said, "sees snakes,"
  When Carver, their own poet, drops the shears,
(The bard's Sub-Editor—fate makes mistakes),
  And in a magazine sheds lyric tears;
Their Bowman, too, a wondrous name has got,
Though it does not appear what he has shot.

LIX.

They've publishers who print railway reports,
  And so, of course, are guides to literature;
They 've journalists who do the County Courts,
  And know the *Times'* great guns, and tell you who're
The authors of the "Coming K——"; all sorts
  Of Lilliputians, empty and obscure,
Swell out here twice a week, and, lulled by shag,
Dream that they're citizens of Brobdingnag.

LX.

"That 's old Bohemia," said Jon Duan's guide,
  "Impotent, gouty, full of age and spite;
Let's leave them o'er their whisky to decide
  Browning's a bubble, Morris is a mite,
And only Ashby Sterry opens wide
  A window on the starry infinite.
Come westward—there's Bohemia, young and sunny,
With no gray hairs—and generally no money."

LXI.

I want an Invocation, for the theme
  Is one of that sublime and solemn kind
That ought to be approached with half a ream
  Of "Ohs" addressed to deities, designed
To give us time to invent and get up steam,
  And tune our fiddles ere we raise the blind—
Also to make the publisher advance a
Pound or two more 'cause of the extra stanza.

LXII.

But really I find nothing to invoke.
  Before the Great Apollo Club, the Muses
Shrink back, and blushes clothe them as a cloak;
  Venus, Diana, Jupiter refuses.
Priapus might do, but much finer folk
  Retain his services; one picks and chooses—
But, faith, the naughtiest gods in Lemprière,
Are quite surpassed in Hanoveria Square.

LXIII.

So let the chaste Apollo Club be seen
  Without vain dallying at the modest door;
Follow Jon Duan and Maloy between
  Two rows of hats, and pictures, which all bore
The impress of free minds that scorned to screen
  The beauties Nature meant us to adore:
Here they'd corrupt, such thin toilettes enwrap 'em,
The seminaries most select in Clapham.

LXIV.

Upstairs, a lively circle is fulfilling
  The promise of the pictures—that's to say,
Divesting truth of all the flounce and frilling,
  That so disguise her in the present day;
And in our "cleanly English tongue" * instilling
  The subtle piquancy of Rabelais;
They don't mince words here—if they did they'd hurry
To put in spice, and make the mincemeat—curry.

LXV.

Champagne and seltzer corks are popping gaily;
  It's two o'clock; the night has just begun;
In pour the critics from the theatres, palely,
  Suffering from Byron's or Burnand's last pun.

* An idiom of the *Daily Telegraph.*

Here comes Fred Bates, who dines with Viscounts
  daily,
And hatches "high life" novels by the ton;
Here's the sleek Jew band leader, Knight — and
  then,
One "Gentleman who writes for Gentlemen."

LXVI.
Smoke, and a rivulet of seltz. and brandy;
  A buzz of talk that oft becomes a roar;
Impassive waiters setting glasses handy;
  On settees, arm-chairs, lounging, some three-
    score
Tenors and poets, dramatists and dandy
  Diplomatists and dilettanti; four
Painters who've coloured nothing but a pipe,
Because the Royal Academy's not ripe

LXVII.
For philosophic realism; a common
  Creature or two, who neither wrote nor drew,
And whom, therefore, the Club expects to summon
  Up fierce enthusiasm for the men who do—
Clerks from the War Office, who love to strum on
  Their red-tape lyres, and think they're poets too;
A Communist freed from Versailles inquisitors—
They make a point of showing him to visitors.

LXVIII.
There's a broad line fire of buffoonery,
  There are the single cracks of paradox;
Here, splutters from the whip of Irony;
  And cynicism's icy ooze that mocks
One moment, the last moment's deity :—
  An intellectual Babel, that oft shocks
At first the pious stranger, and confuses—
That's how most of us cultivate the Muses.

LXIX.
Jon Duan promptly made himself at home.
  He'd just such erudition as they prize
At the Apollo Club : he'd read Brantôme,
  Faublas, and Casanova—which supplies
A man with many anecdotes and some
  Vices; but here it served to make him rise
In favour with his friends, who won't deny
Their library is very like a sty.

LXX.
As dawn approached, the conversation grew
  More lyrical : they passed the loving cup;
They felt all men were brothers—which is true—
  All Cains and Abels; and, like men who sup
In the small hours, they felt old songs steal through
  The vapours of the wine, and struggle up
Unto the lips. So, finding they grew dreamy, a
Poet trolled this Carol of Bohemia.

A Carol of Bohemia.
1.
Bohemians! this our trade and rank, we drift
  without an anchor,
All idle 'prentices who've broke Society's inden-
  ture;
Gil Blas, whose lives are voyages to some hazy
  Salamanca;—
We'll pit against your L. S. D. our motto : Per-
  adventure.

2.
The hostelries upon our way keep open house and
  table;
And if e'en at the first relay, we find the money
  short,
With muleteers of old romance we sup in barn or
  stable,
And if the bread is black, the wine but vinegar
  —*qu' importe!*

3.
Qu' importe the chasm and precipice, *qu' importe*
  too, death and danger!
We take the truant's path in life, and there one
  never slips.
If all the men we meet are foes, there's not a girl a
  stranger,
When one has Murger in the heart, and Musset
  on the lips!

4.
O, green ways trodden hand in hand ! O sweet
  things that mean nothing !
And Raphael's fair sister, who makes vagrant
  hearts beat louder.
Ah, for the golden spring of life ! Ah, for the
  autumn loathing !—
Raphael robs the traveller, Madonna's plumes
  are powder.

5.

And russet comes upon the green; we see the
    roses' canker;
Lorenza's little hands I hold have trenchant tips
    and scar mine,
Gil Blas grows fat and falls asleep, half-way to
    Salamanca;
And Laura's kisses are so sweet—they make
    one's moustache carmine!

LXXI.

As the last echoes into stillness sunk,
    Jon Duan rose and bade adieu to Babel;
He'd seen and heard enough; his ideal shrunk
    Within him, and he felt his gods unstable;
He left a famous poet very drunk,
    Reciting bits from Pindar, on the table;
And others, dry as wither'd leaves in Arden,
To finish up the night at Covent Garden.

LXXII.

These are the ordeals through which greenhorns
    pass
Before they're fit to form public opinion,
Or in romance to hold up a clear glass
    To modern men and manners; their dominion
Is reached by by-ways tortuous and crass,
    Wherein one's pure ambition moults its pinion,
And changes so in heart and aim and soul—
What was an eagle dwindles to poor poll.

LXXIII.

They set forth with their poems in their wallet,
    And nothing much to speak of in their purse,
Thinking they're going to wield Thor's mighty
    mallet,
    And all the bubbles of the age disperse;
Proud of their Mission, as the poor lads call it—
    To mend the world in philosophic verse,
To speak out boldly, giving stout all-rounders,
From Vested Interests unto Pious Founders;

LXXIV.

To laugh to scorn our wars of sacristies,
    That set us flying at each other's throats,
Because some curates like gay draperies,
    Or rather higher collars to their coats:—
And then they bandy talk of "heresies"—
    That's what the beams denominate the motes,—
Set doctors arguing and lawyers fighting—
And, one good thing, set Mr. Gladstone writing;

LXXV.

To tilt against—but who shall give the list
    Of all the wrongs and ills that want redressing
In this sweet isle, where, if a sore exist,
    Fourscore-year bishops say it's a great blessing?
Who'll count the reefs and rocks seen through the
    mist,
    Through which Pangloss, M.P., says we're pro-
    gressing?
Who'll count our paupers, plutocrats—none can
    aver—
And oh! who'll count the Royal House of Hanover?

LXXVI.

One thought that one could do it all, elated
    With young dreams, when life's morning star
    its best shone;
Political economy we rated
    Merely the art of sidling round the question:—
St. Giles's hunger isn't compensated
    Or cured by Lord St. James's indigestion:
And then we found blank looks on either hand—
St. Giles can't read—St. James can't understand.

LXXVII.

And all our wings fell from us, and we stumbled,
    Crawled crablike, sneaked, and sidled with the
    best;
Exalted Toole, Vance, H.R.H.s,—humbled
    Your Arch's, Bradlaughs, Odgers, and the rest;
We hung on to Fame's chariot as it rumbled
    Down Fleet Street—and from that day, were well
    dressed,
And had a cheque-book—knew a peer who pities
Us scribes, and sat on several Club Committees.

LXXVIII.

An old, old tale: a lucky hero ours,
    To have it all made plain before he started
On that road, which seems carpeted with flowers
    To amateurs who're young and simple hearted;
He grieved at first, and, for a few brief hours,
    His eyes, because the scales had dropp'd off,
    smarted;
But soon he hardened into crying, Bosh!—
Couleur de rose—that colour doesn't wash!

LXXIX.

And he went in for all the browns and grays
    Of stern reality, for perfect prose

In life, in literature, in aims, and ways:
  He came to know the fact that no man goes
To market with an ingot: bread or bays,
  Small change will buy the best that's baked or
    grows.
He sent his grand old idols to the mint—
And rich and godless, soon prepared to print.

LXXX.

You've seen his progress in the magazines,
  Reviews and Quarterlies ; his course is planned
After the best authorities, on means
  Whereby to keep one's name before the land :
To start with, his identity he screens,
  Forthwith, a weekly says: "We understand
The paper in this month's 'True Blue,' which
    no one
Failed to remark, is written by Jon Duan."

LXXXI.

Or ere the paper's printed : "We're informed
  The 'Unicorn' for next month will contain
An essay by Jon Duan." Thus he charmed
  The public with reiterative strain,
Till simple outsiders grew quite alarmed
  At the prodigious business of his brain ;
And he grew known so, he'd a near escape
From having his fine features limned by "Ape."

LXXXII.

And to their country cousins Cockneys said :
  "Pray notice! look! he's passing! that is he!
That noble presence—that inspirèd head—
  Lit by the dawn of young celebrity—
That is Jon Duan, following up the thread
  Of his new serial for the 'Busy Bee,'
Or gleaning bits of realism in the gutter,
That's what makes his romance go down like
    butter."

LXXXIII.

And stern reviewers softened as he passed,
  And lo! were nearly men.—He gave small
    dinners,
Into which all Fin-Bec's menus were cast,
  And unto which he bade—as should beginners—
The baldest critics, editors, and fast
  War correspondents, with sweet little sinners
(Such things divert the labours of the desk),
Whose rôle is Legs in every new burlesque.

LXXXIV.

No bribes! Thank Heaven, the English press is
    pure ;—
A model for all Europe, and a score tall
  Yankees ! but sometimes salaries aren't secure ;—
And sometimes even journalists are mortal ;
  Therefore a little dinner-card, when you're
In want of praise, will open many a portal ;—
I'd name—if libel cases weren't so brisk—
A dozen laurel wreaths that sprung from *bisque*.

LXXXV.

Laurels Jon Duan got, or substitutes
  For what they called wreaths eighty years ago :
Success in our days yields more solid fruits
  Than figurative chaplets—fruits that grow
Too quickly, maybe, and from rotten roots,
  But still afford a pleasant meal or so.
And after all, to make a crop secure,
Don't the best cultivators use manure?

LXXXVI.

We don't say that Jon Duan did ; he merely
  Knew his age well, and catered for its taste.
It loves the portrait of its vices dearly,
  Provided certain angles are effaced,
And certain details not described too clearly—
  A photograph half libertine, half chaste,
That matrons smile at, and girls in their teens
Say prettily they can't see what it means.

LXXXVII.

That is our "social, psychologic" fiction,
  In which Grub Street takes vengeance on Bel-
    gravia,
Denouncing all its sins with feigned affliction
  At having to describe the bad behaviour
Of titled folks—for there's an interdiction
  On vulgar crimes ; we treat those that are caviar
Unto the general—pigeon-shooting, gaming,
Genteel polygamy—*all* won't bear naming.

LXXXVIII.

And this Jon Duan painted to the life.
  Ne'er was a better writer to portray
Thoroughbreds, cocottes, and post-nuptial strife,
  And scenery in a pretty Mignard way ;
To show how one makes love to a friend's wife,
  Or leads a virgin's timid steps astray,—

How to transgress the Ten Commandments daily,
Wear good coats well—and *not* end at the Old
    Bailey.

LXXXIX.

He also touched on politics, and wrote
    The usual anonymous report,
From Cloudland allegorical; we dote
    On pamphlets of the Prince Florestan sort,
Putting them down to ten M.P.s of note,
    For lively satire is our statesmen's forte.
Talk of the daily press, Mill, Grote—oh, fiddle!
The best loved flower of literature's a riddle.

XC.

Reviews, translations, travels, essays, stories,
    Liberal programmes, letters to the *Times*—
The record of his exploits would crack Glory's
    Trumpet, unused to praise *this* kind of crimes;
Each week the acid Athenæum bore his
    Name in some column, linked to prose or rhymes,
Which being largely advertised and often,
Made the most stony critic's bosom soften.

XCI.

No evanescent Period was founded,
    Or foundered, but he had his finger in it;
No Mirror crack'd, no Junius fell down dead,
    No Torch illumed the country for a minute,
But in their columns his MS. abounded;
    Eclecticism was his prevailing sin, it
Led him to promise prose to that transcendent
Modern press joke: The Daily Independent!

XCII.

That crowns a man's career; no further goes
    The force of sane ambition. For the rest,
He'd all the wealth of privilege one owes
    To having frequently in print express'd
Old thoughts about some older joys and woes
    He had his stalls for nothing, and the best
Place on first nights—a manager's civility,
Which is the author's patent of nobility.

XCIII.

He had the run of philosophic bars,
    Where literature's professors congregate,
With haply, some clean-shaven tragic stars,
    And a few faithful servants of the State,
Who make enough to pay for their cigars,
    By writing critiques for the press—a fate
So few sane men in our days seem to covet—
Thank God! the Civil Service ain't above it.

XCIV.

The damsels who deign serve you with your beer
  Are deeply versed in literature and art ;
And oh! the things those virgins see and hear
  Would rather make the goddess Grundy start.
It's not improving always to sit near
  Authors, who, if they don't attack your heart,—
For they can't touch it, though they've won some laurels—
Do play the very devil with your morals.

XCV.

Wide as they range, a flavour of sour ink
  Goes with them, from the City to the Strand,
And thence to Panton Street. Just watch them pink
  A reputation with a master-hand ;
List to them squabbling, and observe them drink—
  And then reflect, to-morrow all the land
Will only know which way the world's inclining,
By what they all have put into their "lining."

XCVI.

Leave them. The Muse, poor jade, has had her fill
  Of copy and of copy writers. Satis,
Even Jon Duan, though he's prosperous, still
  Cries now and then, when he sees what his fate is—
To grind for ever in the same old mill
  The same old thoughts, for evermore to mate his
Dreams with the need of publishers and editors—
Because the Ideal won't appease one's creditors.

XCVII.

Leave them, and leave Jon Duan for awhile,
  One of their band, a brother—till one sees
A way that's safe to say his prose is vile,
  And his successes only plagiaries ;

You'll meet them all to-morrow and you'll smile
  At their old jokes, weep o'er their elegies,
Admire them all in copy which encumbers
The New Year Annuals and the Christmas Numbers.

XCVIII.

We've seen Jon Duan through Grub Street, safe and sound—
  The passage isn't always so secure :
Footpads are plenty, publishers abound—
  Things which don't tend to keep a young man pure.
We've seen him fêted, published, bought and crowned,
  And shown at all Smith's bookstalls : now he's sure
Of immortality—and, such is fame—
Forty years hence, e'en Timbs won't know his name.

XCIX.

'Tis the best way to leave a hero—great,
  The friend of critics, prosperous and fat ;
Keeping his brougham, asked to civic fêtes,
  And noble poets' garden parties.—That
Is not invariably an author's fate,
  But we want an exception, for thereat
The amateurs take fire, write verse by scores—
And that's the way to punish editors.

C.

And so he's reached the glorious apogee ;
  And success has no history ;—like Peace,
He's at an altitude whereunto we
  Can't follow, for our wings are fixed with grease,
And in the sun's red rays shake wofully :
  But his will prove he's found the golden fleece :
We lei.. v. him, with a set, refined and manly,
Talking of Gladstone's pamphlet with Dean Stanley.

Canto The Fourth.

I.

ST. PAUL once had apartments with a tanner,—
  The street, you may remember, was called Straight,—
But whether Peter lodged in such a manner,
  The pens of the Apostles don't relate:
We know he'd several blots upon his banner,
  And that he now keeps guard at Heaven's gate:
But as to what his social habits were,
The details we can find are very rare.

II.

Though we are bound our full belief to give
  To that sad business about the Cock;
And though that other incident will live—
  When he gave Malchus such a sudden shock.—
Our information's mostly negative
  'Bout this Barjona, who was christened "Rock";
Yet we're inclined to think Pierre a hearty,
Hot-temper'd, bold, and fearless sort of party.

III.

He readily gave up his little all—
  The fishing business p'rhaps was slow just then—
And, feeling he for preaching had a call,
  He went forthwith to fish for souls of men.
The thought of leaving home did not appal,
  And that he gladly went's no wonder, when,
Alike from Matthew, Mark, and Luke, we find
He must have left a mother-in-law behind!

IV.

However, let St. Peter have his due,
  He was a faithful follower, on the whole;
Human, of course—so, equally, are you—
  But he'd a loving and an ardent soul,
Which, after persecutions not a few,
  Bore him in triumph to a martyr's goal;
And left behind him an undying fame,
Heirship to which Rome's Pope advances claim.

V.

Poor Peter! It is monstrously unfair
  That such a Church should take his name in vain;
To say that he first filled the Papal chair
  Must surely give him much *post mortem* pain.

For not his worst detractor could declare
    He e'er did aught the name of Pope to gain.
The lives of few of them will bear inspection;
    For lust and blood most had a predilection.

VI.

And Peter's free from that; he did not fill
    His life with villainies the pen can't write;
His name is not mixed up with crimes that chill;
    With sins incestuous that the soul affright;
He did not torture, persecute, and kill,
    And make his influence a cursing blight;—
When sinning most, he still might have the hope
He'd never sinned enough to be a Pope!

VII.

He ne'er his helpless fellow-creatures robbed,
    To live in sensuality and ease;
He never schemed, and lied, and planned, and jobbed,
    In Heaven's name, his mistresses to please;
His steps were not with guilty favourites mobbed,
    He did not use the Church's holy keys
The door to damned and devilish sins to ope,—
In short, St. Peter never was a Pope!

VIII.

He had no gold nor houses, tithes nor land,
    He had no pictures, and no jewels nor plate;
He never bore a crozier in his hand,
    He never put a mitre on his pate;
He simply followed Jesus Christ's command,
    Which so-called Christians have not done of late;—
Oh! we would raise Hosannahs in our metre,
If pious people were more like St. Peter.

IX.

We will not talk of Rome; its annals black
    Our pages would too deeply, darkly soil;
Upon the Vatican we'll turn our back,
    Lest indignation should too fiercely boil;
Its fiendish crimes have reached a depth, alack!
    T'wards which our feeble pen would vainly toil:
We will not dabble in the dirt of Rome,
We have enough to do to look at home.

X.

Each sect of Christians in numbers grows,
    Who with the nomination are suffic'd;
Who are to what their Founder taught, fierce foes,
    Boasting a bastard creed, with errors spiced.
The Christians of the present day are those
    Whose words and actions savour least of Christ,
And reckon but of very little count
The precepts of the Sermon on the Mount!

XI.

The English Church our serious thought bespeaks—
    We write as friend to it, and not as foeman;
We write to save it from the trait'rous sneaks
    Who, English-named, at heart are wholly Roman;
We write, unfettered, with a pen that seeks
    Fair field from all, favour undue from no man;
We write because a thousand blots besmear
Th' escutcheon of the Church we held so dear.

XII.

Blots of all kinds and colours, sorts and sizes—
    Blots Evangelical and Ritualistic;
Blots so pronounced that indignation rises;
    Blots hidden carefully in language mystic;
Blots publicly exhibited as prizes;
    Blots to all usefulness antagonistic—
Blots so diffuse, in fact, that without doubt
They threaten soon to blot the Church right out.

XIII.

Our hero knew that some such blots existed,
    For he'd an uncle who'd been Bishop made;
The reason being that he for years persisted
    In giving to the Tory party aid.
Though how it was such services could be twisted
    To show a fitness for the Bishop grade,
We've tried to find out, but we've tried in vain—
Perhaps Lord Shaftesbury could this explain.

XIV.

Jon's Bishop-uncle was a portly man,
    With well-filled waistcoat, and a port-wine nose;
Who, since to be a vicar he began,
    Had never seen his watch-seals or his toes;
Who, knowing life to be at best a span,
    Resolved to eat good dinners to its close;
And giving thanks each day to God the giver,
O'erfed himself, and took those pills called liver.

XV.

It did not seem, save as an awful warning,
    He thought of the directions Christ had given;
His Purse was large; he search'd the *Times* each
    morning,
That he might see how well his Scrip had thriven
Was far from bed-accommodation scorning,
    And never walked it, when he could be driven.
And if the meek in heart alone are bless'd,
He must for cursing long have been assessed.

XVI.

He hunger'd and he thirsted, it is true—
    But not for Righteousness—it is most clear.
He mourn'd—but that was merely 'cause he knew
    A neighbouring Bishop had more pounds a year;
He laid up earthly treasures not a few,
    But of the moth and rust he had no fear;
And whilst of meat and drink he took much
    thought,
Consider'd not the lilies as he ought.

XVII.

In sooth, Jon Duan could not find a trait
    In which the Bishop followed the Great Master;
His diocese brought £15 a day,
    And he contriv'd to make a fortune faster
Than money-changers, for he'd a 'cute way
    Of speculating that ne'er met disaster;—
And as his will proved, later, it is gammon
To think one cannot worship God and Mammon.

XVIII.

Of course he something did his pay to earn:
    He wrote a bitter book against Dissent;
And once a year, in May, his soul would burn,
    Because the Hindoo had no Testament;
And to the House of Lords his feet would turn,
    If by his aid reforms he could prevent:
And he'd some trouble, too, in duly giving
To all his reverend relatives a living!

XIX.

He has in Ember * weeks to lay his hands
    Upon the candidates for ordination;
In his be-puffed lawn sleeves, and linen bands,
    He 'mongst the ladies makes no small sensation;

    * It is not singular perhaps that Ember week is prolific in "sticks."

And periodic'lly his lordship stands
To consummate the rite of confirmation,
Which, being an Epicure, he finds not easy,
For as a rule the children's heads are greasy.

XX.

And shame to say, this pillar of the Church
Is the severest landlord in the county ;
Woe to the tenant, who, left in the lurch,
Is not quite ready with the right amount ; he
Gets no mercy, for the strictest search
Reveals no instance of this Bishop's bounty—
Bounty, indeed, ne'er enters in his plans,
Except it is that Bounty called Queen Anne's !

XXI.

Meantime, whilst this good man in wealth is rolling,
His slaving curates scarce get bread to eat ;
As he his soul with choice old wine's consoling
(Fit follower of the Apostles' feet !),
They, as their wretched stipend they are doling
(The Bishop in three months spends more in meat),
Must recollect, although it seems odd, rather,
That he, in God, is their Right Reverend Father.

XXII.

How very strange it is that Mr. Miall
Won't let a state of things like this alone !
For him to say the Church is on its trial
Is but mere foolery, we all must own ;
The Bench of Bishops cannot fail to smile,—
The Church they grace is steadfast as the throne,—
" Ged rid of us indeed, what nonsense ! Zounds!
We cost each year two hundred thousand pounds !"

XXIII.

The Bishops ! What a volume in a word !
Our hearts beat quicker at the very sound ;
Get rid of them, indeed !—it's too absurd.
Shame on the men who such a scheme propound !
Oh ! can it be that they have never heard
How in good works the Bishops all abound ?
Let Science, Art, and Learning pass away,
But leave us Bishops to crown Coming K——.

Our Bishops.

1.

Who follow Christ with humble feet,
And rarely have enough to eat,
Who " Misereres " oft repeat ?—
Our Bishops.

2.

Who, like the fishermen of old,
Care not for house, nor lands, nor gold,
But boldly brave the damp and cold ?—
Our Bishops.

3.

Who preach the gospel to the poor,
And nurse the sick, and teach the boor—
Who faithful to the end endure ?—
Our Bishops.

4.

Who give up all for Jesus' sake,
And no thought for the morrow take,
But daily sacrifices make ?—
Our Bishops.

5.

And who count everything a loss
Except their Lord and Master's cross,
And reckon riches as but dross ?—
Our Bishops.

XXIV.

Thus Duan sings as he one night is dining
With his good Bishop-uncle *tête à tête* ;
What time the prelate's nose is redly shining,
And brightly gleams his bald and polished pate.
He does not speak, they had some time been wining,
Yet on his face is satisfaction great ;
And when his nephew the decanter passes,
They toast the Bench of Bishops in full glasses.

XXV.

Let's leave the reverend Epicure to fuddle ;
Of many bishop-types he is but one ;
And who can wonder at the Church's muddle,
When half a dozen ways its leaders run ?
When some are smeared with Babylonish ruddle,
And some are steeped in Evangelic dun;
When Broad and High Church meet in battle-shocks,
And Low Church pelts the pair of them with *Rocks*.

XXVI.

Meantime, whilst High and Narrow, Low and Broad,
   And Deep (the Deep are those who get the prizes)
All fight together, for the praise of God,
   The thought in some few people's minds arises,
Why any longer they the land defraud ;
   And common-sense most certainly advises
That if their zeal for fighting's so intense,
They ought to do it at their own expense.

XXVII.

For who takes interest in their petty quarrels?
   Who cares for what they wear or how they stand ;
Let the big babies have their bells and corals,
   And play the fool ; but men the right demand
To say these "posers" shall not teach us morals,
   Nor be upheld by law throughout the land.
'Tis time, indeed, the Church to roughly handle,
And stop what has become a crying scandal.

XXVIII.

When Christian Bishops do but bark and bite
   In silly speeches and in unread books ;
When shepherds leave their flocks in sorry plight,
   And lay about them with their pastoral crooks ;
When Congress breaks up in a smart, free fight,
   The state of things delay no longer brooks,
But every day makes the impression stronger—
We should support the Church's wars no longer.

XXIX.

Nor must we in our midst still go on breeding
   A set of priests both pestilent and prying ;
Who, on our daughters' superstitions feeding,
   The strongest bonds of home-love are untying ;
At whose attacks morality is bleeding,
   And Englishwomen's honour lies a-dying—
Who are reviving, with zeal retrogressional,
The grievous scandals of the old confessional.

XXX.

These fellows are the worst ;—not half so bad
   The Calvinists who say we must be damned,
Nor those who go at times revival mad,
   And glory in conversions that are shamm'd ;
Nor those who, Spurgeon apeing, think to add
   To their renown by getting churches cramm'd,
Nor think how much they let religion down
By posturing weekly as a pulpit clown.

XXXI.

A truce, though—we are getting very prosy,
   And quite forgetting our long-suffering hero.
For the long sermon to atone, suppose he
   Appear at once and dance a gay bolero,
Or sing a ditty, amorous and rosy,
   To bring our readers' spirits up from zero—
Or stay, what's better still, let us prevail
On him to tell a Ritualistic tale.

Jon Duan's Tale.

A STORY OF THE CONFESSIONAL.

1.

Know ye the place where they press and they hurtle,
And do daring deeds for greed and for gain,
Where the mellow milk-punch and the green-fatted turtle
Now mildly digest, and now madden with pain?
Know ye the land of Stone and of Vine,
Where mayors ever banquet and aldermen dine;
Where Emma was wooed, and Abbott laid low,
And they fly paper kites and big bubbles blow;
Where Gold is a god unassail'd in his might,
And neck-ties are loosened when stocks get too tight?
If this district you know—it is E.C. to guess,
And you go up a street which the Hebrews possess,
And turn to the right,—why, then, for a wager,
You come to the Church of St. Wackslite the Major;
And list, as o'er noises that constantly swell,
Comes the soul-stirring sound of its evensong bell.

2.

Robed in the vestments of the East,
Apparell'd as becomes a priest,
Awaiting his sacristan's knock,
The Rev'rend Hippolytus Stock
Sat musing in his vestry chair.

Deep thought was on his pasty face,
His tonsured head was racked with care;—
A smell of spirits filled the place—
(Terrestrial spirits such as we
Call mystic'ly Brett's O. D. V.)
His crafty soul, well skill'd to hide,
The guilty secrets kept inside,
Could smoothe not from his furrow'd brow
The anxious lines that seared it now.

3.

'Twas strange what troubled him, he had
All things that Ritualists make glad:
Embroider'd banners, silken flags,
And velvet Offertory Bags:
Two Utrecht Altar-cloths with lace,
Font Jugs and Buckets in their place.
Of Candlesticks a wondrous pair,
A Chalice Veil of texture rare.
Rich Dossals in the chancel hang;
From Carven Desks the choir-boys sang
The Pavement was encaustic tiles;
The Fauld Stools of the latest styles.
Even the Hat-suspenders show'd
The latest ritualistic *mode;*
His Maniples were fair and white;
His Sacramental Spoons a sight;
The Chancel nothing could surpass,
The Altar-rails were polish'd brass;
Assorted Crosses every where,
Assist the congregation's prayer;
Indeed, though it involved some loss,
The Napkins* were cut on the cross;
He'd Cutters for the sacred bread;
And from an Eagle lectern read;
The Pews were new, the Windows stained,—
In short, no single want remained,
Suggested by religious pride,
Which had not promptly been supplied.
So 'twas no use to go again
To Cox and Sons in Maiden Lane.—
Yet still those reverend features bore
The anxious look we've named before.

4.

The knock was heard, a form appear'd,
A black, lank form with copious beard—
"Three minutes, and the bell will cease."
Then, Hippolytus, "Hold thy peace!
Has the communion plate been clean'd?"
The lank one acquiescence lean'd—
"Three boys," he said, "have work'd for hours,
Gard's Plate Cloth capitally scours,
I never saw it look so bright,
You *will* feel proud of it to-night."
"And has that sack of incense come?"
The lank one, save for "Yes," was dumb.

---

   * A friend who thinks all Ritualists are vipers,
     These napkins christens "Ritualistic Wipers."

"Incense is up again, beware!
The Acolytes must take more care.
They burn too much of it at nights."
  And here the black form silence brake—
"O, Sir, concerning those wax lights:
  Wicks says he will a discount make
On thirty pounds for ready cash."
The vicar smiled, he was not rash,
  And merely murmuring softly, "Thirty?"
Continued in a louder tone,
  "Joseph, that I. H. S. is dirty,
See by a sister it is scrubbed,
And have my pocket-service rubbed.
And say to Mrs. Sniggs, it's bosh!
That Alb did *not* come from the wash.
And now, enough of worldly cares,
Lead on the way to evening prayers!"

5.

St. Wackslite's filled with floods of light,
'Tis celebration high to-night.
The organ peals, the people kneels.
The "supers" first their banners bear,
The vergers with their wands are there,
The choristers march two by two,
The Acolytes their duties do.
And as their censers high are sway'd,
They would a sweet perfume have made,
Had not the incense been of late
Cheap, truly,—but adulterate.

Lay brothers in due sequence walk,
The assistant-priests behind them stalk.
Last comes in robes which rainbows mock
The Reverend Hippolytus Stock;
And round the church in order slow,
They with triumphal music go.
But by the door a son of sin,
  A writer in the rabid *Rock*,
Has managed early to slip in—
  'Tis his to cause a sudden shock.
For in a tone so full and clear
That everyone cannot but hear,
His voice he raises and recites
These lines, and not a line but bites:—

      The Aisles of Rome.
           I.
"The aisles of Rome! the aisles of Rome!
  Where burning censers oft are swung,

Where saints are worshipp'd 'neath the dome,
  Where banners sway and mass is sung—
In Papal Sees these aisles have place,
  But English churches they disgrace.

II.

" The vestments, many-hued and quaint,
  The alb, the stole, the hood, the cope,
The prayers to Virgin and to saint—
  These are for them who serve the Pope :
Shame ! that such mummeries besmirch
  The ritual of the English Church !

III.

" I took the train to Farringdon,
  From Farringdon I walked due E. ;
And musing there an hour alone,
  I scarce could think such things could be.
At Smithfield—scene of martyrs slain—
  I could not deem they died in vain.

IV.

" And is it so ? and can it be,
  My country ? Is what we deplore
Aught but a phase of idiocy ?
  Is England Protestant no more ?
Is she led captive by a man—
  The dotard of the Vatican ?

V.

" Must we but weep o'er days more blest ?
  Must we but blush ?—Our fathers bled.
Earth, render back from out thy breast
  A remnant of our martyred dead !
Of all the hundreds grant but three
  To fight anew Mackonochie."

This while had all around been dazed,
  And no one tried his tongue to stay ;
The choristers had ceased, amazed,
  The organ did no longer play.
But soon a sense of wrong return'd,
  And scores of eager fingers burn'd
To turn the ribald traitor out ;
  And there arose a shaming shout,
And several vergers for him made ;
  Still he no sign of fear betrayed.
In truth, so full of zeal was he,
  Another verse he did begin,
But, promptly fetched, P.C. 9 E.
  Appears, and forthwith "runs him in."

The organ then peals forth once more,
And the processional is o'er.

6.

The three assistant priests await
    The signal to officiate,
And bide till 'tis their vicar's will
    To dance the usual quadrille.
Then, when he joins their little band,
And all before the altar stand,
They face the east, they face the west,
They face the ways that please them best;
They scuffle quickly *dos-à-dos*,
And through gymnastic motions go;
They turn to corners, do the chain,
Kneel down, get up, and kneel again;
The vicar, plainly as can be,
Makes an exemplary M.C.
Each tangled move he regulates,
And juggles with the cups and plates—
No slip, no stumble, not a fault;
Though he is near two-score and fat,
He could have turned a somersault,
This Ritualistic acrobat.
Nay, it obtains among his friends,
    And is in Low Church circles said,
That Hippolytus soon intends
    To celebrate "upon his head!"

7.

The organ plays its final note,
    The church is wrapp'd in silent gloom,
A dreamy stillness seems to float,
    The vicar seeks his robing-room.
One duty now remains for him,
    'Tis the Confessional to seek,
Where burns the waxen taper dim,
    And hear the heart-thoughts of the weak.
And, as he goes, he murmurs low,
    "Yes! she will come, for she was there!"
And in his eyes hot passions glow,
    As sits he in his oaken chair.
And now, one parts the curtains red,
And kneels, and bows a guilty head,
With many a tale of sin and woe;
Still others come, and kneel, and go—
Escaping thus, they think, the ban
Shed o'er them by this wicked man.
His eyes still peer with anxious care,
He mutters, "Surely she was there!"

Then fiendish lustre fills his eyes,
And colour to his pale cheeks flies,
For down the aisle, in the light so dim,
A female form comes straight to him,
And he knows by the hat with the sea-gull's wing,
    And the cuirass cut in the latest fashion,
That those faintly-falling footsteps bring
    The woman he loves with a guilty passion.

8.

Thoughts of the past rush through his brain,
Thoughts rapturous, yet link'd with pain,
    Of the sweet face when first she came
    His spiritual aid to claim—
Of her soft arms, in meekness bending
    Across her maiden's budding breast;
Of those soft arms anon extending
    To clasp the hands of him who blest.
O she was fair! her eyes were blue,
    Her hair was golden, as spun sunbeams are;
Her cheeks had robbed the rosebuds of their hue,
    Her voice was music coming from afar;
And she, suspecting naught, was full of trust—
    Trust, confidence and innocence inspire;
Whilst he look'd on her lovely form and bust,
    And vow'd to win her to his fierce desire.
Yes, she was fair as first of womankind,
    When in her virgin innocence first smiling;
And he, with cruel purpose in his mind,
    Was wily as the serpent; her beguiling
With holy words and hypocritic speeches,
Such as the Ritualistic manual teaches.

    Too many times she came, and he
        Plied her with subtle Jesuitry;
    Poison'd her mind and soil'd her heart
        With all his cunning, priestly art;
    Dealing his every venomed stroke
        From underneath religion's cloak,
    Till, counting her within his power,
    He hailed th' approach of triumph's hour,
    And, as her frail form meets his sight,
    He plans her fall that very night.

9.

In silence bow'd the virgin's head;
    As if her eyes were fill'd with tears,
That stifled feeling dared not shed—
    As if o'ercome by maiden's fears.

"My daughter!" quoth the wicked priest,
"Your face lift up, tell me, at least,
What ghostly trouble rives your soul—
God gives me power to make it whole."
And, as he spoke, behind her head
He closely drew the curtains red;
But still no word her silence broke,
Her presence sighs alone bespoke.
"My daughter!" thus the priest again,
"Your studied reticence is vain."
His lips bent forward near her ear,
"Come, cast away your foolish fear;
Confess the sins that on you press—
Confess to me, sweet girl, confess!"
Save heavier sighs, no answer came,
 The vicar's breath came quicklier, then—
"Dear Alice!"—for he knew her name—
Burst forth that villain amongst men,
"I quite forget my own distress
 In telling you I love you well,—
So well, that all the pains of Hell
I'd bear for one long, close caress."
No movement yet. "O, Alice, make
Some answer, lest my heart should break.
I am your priest, I know your heart;
Alice, I will not from you part.
I've sworn to be a celibate,
And marriage vows are not for me;
But holy love and passion great
A mingled fate for us decree.
I claim you, who shall dare say nay,
Or tear you from my arms away?
Come, darling, we are all alone,
One hour will all past pain atone;
Come, let no longer aught divide—
Come, darling, be the Church's bride!"

10.

All suddenly the female form arose,
And as the vicar stretched his arms to seize her,
A manly fist dash'd right into his nose,
 A crushing blow, call'd vulgarly a "sneezer";
And whilst he felt all nose and strange surprise,
 The fist work'd piston-like just twice or thrice,
And bunged up straightway were his sunken eyes,
 And then his throat was seized as in a vice.
Whilst, as his breath was being shaken out,
 And he felt he would very quickly smother—
Then, just before he fainted, came a shout,
 Of "Alice could not come! but I'm her brother!"

11.

The Reverend Hippolytus Stock
 Was kept for several weeks in bed;
It was a very sudden shock,
 And very copiously he bled.
He suffered very dreadful pain,
 His mental torture was still greater;
His nose will ne'er be straight again,—
 Let's hope his notions will be straighter!

XXXII.

Thus told, or would, or could, or should have told
 Our hero Duan, in tolerable rhyme,
The story of the Ritualist, so sold,
 A precious product of this popish time.
Such men o'er wives and daughters get a hold,
 Combining snake-like venom with its slime.—
Jon knew the details well; he was no other
Than the revenging metamorphosed brother.

XXXIII.

He'd seen his sister mope for weeks and weeks,
 And grow more melancholy every day;
He half suspected Ritualistic freaks,
 Knowing her inclinations went that way.
At last, her fullest confidence he seeks,
 And learns enough to fill him with dismay;
Then warns her promptly of her wily foe,
And lays the stratagem of which you know.

XXXIV.

When all his sister's clothes he had put on,
 And sought from paint and tweezers artful aid,
No casual glance could have detected Jon,
 He looked so very like a pretty maid;
And with long tresses his head pinn'd upon,
 A perfect transformation was display'd.
In fact, to Alice, for the parson's liking,
He show'd resemblance very much too striking!

XXXV.

Ex uno disce omnes! 'Tis a saying
 We cannot well too strongly bear in mind—
Beware the clergymen at Popery playing,
 The set to priestly arrogance inclined;
They are, at best, beguiling and betraying
 The sacred ties around our hearts entwined.
Husbands and Brothers! stamp out like small-pox,
Virus that breeds in the Confession-box.

Canto The Fifth.

I.

"HELL is a city (very) much like London"—
  The words are Shelley's, reader, not our own—
If it be so, then there's no lack of Pun done
  Down in that place where Satan has his throne.
Nor would the hardened sinner be quite undone,
  Were he sent there for sinning to atone.
In fact, the Ranters would not make us cry,
If we'd to go to London when we die.

II.

Of course there are two sides to every question,
  There's not a medal has not its obverse—
Good dinners have their following indigestion,
  And London has its bad side and its worse;
But, if we choose the good side and the rest shun,
  Who can our somewhat natural choice asperse?
If Duan chose what he thought best, with zest,
'Tis not for us to say—Bad was his best.

III.

For all these things are matters of opinion—
  And one man's poison is another's meat;
We're not to say a man's the Devil's minion,
  Because no creed he happens to repeat;
Or doom to flames eternal, a Socinian,
  Because One God to him is all complete.
All men have power to choose—by which we mean,
There are such things as moral fat and lean.

IV.

The fat suits one, the lean may suit another;
  And why should we, against our will, eat fat,
Or force the lean on an unwilling brother,
  Who thinks it fit to only feed the cat?
And if a man will eat nor one, nor t'other,
  He surely is best judge what he is at—
No man's a right to, wholly or in part,
Prescribe his brother's moral dinner *carte*.

V.

Wherefore, we say, we will not raise our voice
  To say what Duan chose as best was bad;
He, certainly, did not repent his choice,
  And very rarely was he hipp'd or sad;
Au contraire,—in his youth he did rejoice,
  And who are we that he should not be glad?
He slept well, drank well, ate well, and his dinners
Digested admirably for a sinner's.

VI.

And, by-the-by, what is a sinner, pray?
　"A man who sins." Then, prithee, what is sin?
Let rival sect'ries have on this their say,
　And each a different answer will begin.
Which is confusing, and would cause delay,
　The fact being, we have to look within.
What use are dogmas, doctrines, myths, and creeds?
A man's own heart supplies the truth he needs.

VII.

But these digressions cannot be allow'd,
　Or we shall never tell how Duan fared;
Whilst seeking pleasure in the London crowd—
　How he was pleas'd and flatter'd, trick'd and snared—
But, thanks to his good heart and lineage proud,
　Was yet from every degradation spared.
And how he lived, and went a killing pace,
With polished footsteps and a finished grace.

VIII.

No wonder Duan was a favourite,
　Or that his handsome person was admired;
That he was rather spoilt, if not so quite,
　And that no end of passions he inspired.
It was indeed a trial by no means light
　When he from 'mongst the "upper ten" retired;
And all Society was rather riled
When he took refuge in Bohemia's wild.

IX.

For, he was such a pet, his mirror's frame
　(He had a *suite* of rooms in Piccadilly)
Was studded with the cards with which the game
　Of good Society is played. 'Tis silly
How one admits a piece of pasteboard's claim,
　And has to do its bidding "willy-nilly,"
And dine and dance, and dawdle without measure,
Because it is Society's good pleasure.

X.

No other mistress could be so severe,
　Or bully man so much, or so afflict him,
As Duan found when, in his twentieth year,
　He to her tyranny became a victim;
And served her until, from exhaustion sheer,
　He well-nigh wished Society had kick'd him,
Or that, still better, he had kick'd Society,
And gone in for Bohemian variety.

XI.

Think what he went through! How he'd to observe
　A code of laws unwritten, but Draconic,
Which make life all straight lines without a curve—
　And so conservative and non-Byronic,
That he who from their ruling dares to swerve
　Is punished with severity Masonic—
The eternal laws of Fashion's legislature,
Being ever urged 'gainst those who go for Nature.

XII.

Duan soon found he had to dress by rule;
　His own sartorial taste did not avail; or
Could he help the idea he was a fool
　When he had audiences of his tailor.
Scorn mixed with pity filled the face of Poole
　As he, as though he had been Duan's jailer,
To his directions turned a deaf ear, utter,
And passed him on, unheeded, to the cutter.

XIII.

In vain Jon Duan very mildly states,
　He thinks that pattern and this cut will suit him;
The cutter coolly for his silence waits,
　Nor deigns to take the trouble to refute him;
But, standing sternly to "Le Coupeur" plates,
　Seems as a forward youngster to compute him,
And simply says, as though to save all fuss—
"Gents usually leave such things to us!"

XIV.

We know what that means; for, 'tis no small matter.
　Why do we wear to-day the "chimney-pot"?
Because we leave our head-gear to our hatter,
　And not because one useful point it's got.
Why not the old delusive notion scatter,
　And have a hat not heavy, hard, and hot?—
(That last line, we may make especial mention,
Is worth the Cockney's serious attention.)

XV.

Think of the modern boot, and then say whether
　Such pedal torture must perforce be borne.
Why not encase our feet in untann'd leather,
　And say farewell to blister and to corn?
Let boots and bunions pass away together,
　'Mid universal ecstasy and scorn!
We are but pilgrims, yet, can't there be made
A single "Progress" without "Bunyan's" aid?

XVI.

Must we be always abject slaves, in fact,
    And martyrs to the taste of those who dress us?
Bear meekly all that Fashion does enact
    (She clothes poor woman in a shirt of Nessus!),
And stand, and, like the tailors' dummies, act,
    Whilst into trussed-up blocks our snips compress us?
Free Land! Free Love!—these two cries just now press :
Well, add a third, and clamour for Free Dress!

XVII.

Again, digression! Duan meekly wore
    The clothes his first-class tailors kindly made him;
Bought Hoby's boots, by Lincoln's "stove-pipe" swore;
    And did his hair as Mr. Truefitt bade him:
Had collars, gloves, and useless things galore,
    All which helped in Society to aid him—
And warmly welcomed by Patricia's host,
His name was daily in the *Morning Post.*

XVIII.

Here could be seen—who doubts the *Morning Post?*
    Its articles are like the Thirty-nine—
How often Duan with a noble host
    Would, with more victims, "greatly daring, dine!"
And wonder that, with such parade and boast,
    There was so little food, and such bad wine;
And ask himself, with natural surprise,
If noble hosts fed hunger through the eyes?

XIX.

He dined with Omnium's Duke, that titled rake,
    Who keeps a private house of assignation;
Whose agents, from the West End, nightly take,
    Fresh damsels for his Grace's delectation;
Who, publicly, such efforts seems to make
    For wicked London's moral reformation;
And, as becomes his dignified position,
Is liberal patron of the "Midnight Mission."

XX.

He dined with Earl Tartuffe, who takes the chair,
    When Vice requires his periodic strictures;
And when he dined, saw his collection rare
    Of obscene pamphlets and indecent pictures.

Dined, too, with Lord Cinqfoil, in Blankley Square,
    Who is another of these curious mixtures;
Who has a name and reputation glorious,
Yet takes his neighbours' spoons in way notorious.

XXI.

He put his legs 'neath Lord Macænas' table,
    Who's so much money and so little mind,
Whose sensuality smacks of the stable,
    Though he to Art and Music seems inclined.
He fed with Viscount Quicksot, and was able,
    From after-dinner confidence, to find
The strongest reason why this peer should press
To rescue pretty nurse-girls in distress.

XXII.

He dined at Lambeth Palace with the saints,
    He dined at Richmond (often) with a sinner;
He found that nearly every lady paints,
    And laces far too tight to eat her dinner.
Hidden, in upper circles, he found taints,
    'Neath a disguise that daily waxes thinner.
And that for morals 'tis a very queer age,
And more especially amongst the Peerage.

XXIII.

Yes, 'neath the very dull and placid level,
    He found the morals of high life but lame;
Beneath its mask of etiquette, the Devil
    Promoting scandals that we dare not name.
We'll leave th' *exposé* to some future Greville,
    Nor hurt the fame of any high-born dame—
Though, truth to tell, despite our Sovereign Lady,
Society's repute was ne'er more shady.

XXIV.

The air is full of scandals of divorces,
    The smoking-rooms of Pall Mall reek with rumour;
And if we trace it to its various sources,
    'Tis not, we find, a freak of spite or humour.
No; everywhere demoralizing force is
    Right hard at work; and in a very few more
Years, if there is no change, our upper crust
Will crumble up, destroyed—its lust in dust.

XXV.

At Brookes's, Prince's, at the "Rag" or Raleigh,
    Wherever Duan went, by night or day,
The conversation turned, methodically,
    Upon patrician damsels gone astray;

And scarce an anecdote or witty sally,
 But took a woman's character away.
Titled transgressions seemed the only fashion;
And joys, unblessed by Church, the ruling passion.

XXVI.

But on the surface, as has been expressed,
 Society was placid as before,
And called, and rode, and drove, and "drummed,"
 and dressed,
 As though it had at heart no cancerous sore;
And Duan, being so much in request,
 Full often entered its portentous door,
And, with a Spartan heroism, danced,
Or tea'd at five o'clock with air entranced.

XXVII.

He went to many a hostess's "At home"—
 Where everybody is so much abroad—
Through crammed-up halls and *salons* doomed to
 roam,
 Where, 'spite the heat, the etiquette's not thaw'd;
Up crowded staircases he slowly clomb,
 Hustled and pushed, and trodden on and
 claw'd;—
Such inconvenience much too great a price is
To pay for cold weak tea and lukewarm ices.

XXVIII.

Or e'en to hear the last new baritone,
 Or shake the hand of the receiving Duchess,
Or see the Heir-Apparent to the Throne,
 Trotted round proudly in her eager clutches;
Or catch some flirting matron all alone,
 And make a future assignation; much is
This last in vogue; it is not hard to chouse
The husbands, specially if in the "House."

XXIX.

They go, dear innocents! and sit and snore,
 And vote to order in St. Stephen's Chapel;
Nor dream that gallant captains haunt their door,
 And Princes with their wives' fair virtue
 grapple;
And—well, our womankind are as of yore,
 They have not changed since Eve devoured
 the apple,—
But, 'twould be "rough" on Hannen, past all
 doubt,
If half the husbands found their spouses out.

XXX.

It is not strange that, since our women marry
   For riches and position, name and fame,
They seek for love elsewhere, and quickly carry
   A fierce flirtation on with some old "flame,"
And freely yield to Dick, or Tom, or Harry,
   The pleasant leisure-hours their lords should claim.
And Duan found, when once well in the swim,
His friends' wives made too many calls on him.

XXXI.

Whilst his friends' husbands, not to be outdone,
   Kept pretty, painted cages in "The Wood";
With pretty birdies in them, full of fun,
   And often in a rather naughty mood;—
Thus is it that the double trick is done.
   (To speak such facts is, as we know, tabooed;
But we, spite Mrs. Grundy's interfering,
Intend to strip off modern life's veneering.)

XXXII.

It's very thin, you scratch the Politician,
   And find that he's a hungerer for place;
The great Philanthropist—he makes admission
   His motives would his character disgrace;
The Bishop—and he mourns that his position
   Does not admit that he should go the pace—
Removes from yon Prude's face her veil, so thin,
And, with a leer, she'll lure you into sin.

XXXIII.

Pull off the Church's gown, and she will stand
   A greedy tyrant, gorged with guilt and gold;
Take from Justitia's eyes the blinding band,
   And see her wink as truth is bought and sold;
The mask from Thespis snatch with sudden hand,
   And then in every London stage behold
A mart for painted women, and an aid
To padded Cyprians to ply their trade.

XXXIV.

Pull—no, please don't, on reconsideration!
   Our hero's patient, but to keep him waiting,
While we indulge in moral observation,
   Is calculated to be irritating.
Besides, we have some further information
   To give you of his later doings, dating
From those days when both wiser grown and older,
He gave Society the frigid shoulder.

XXXV.

All her reputed pleasures he had tasted,
   And found them, oft repeated, apt to pall
Upon his palate; he no longer hasted
   To get an invite for the Prince's ball,
And thought the hours were altogether wasted
   He spent in evening routs and morning call;
And even found, in time, to care one fails
'Bout meeting Him of Cambridge or of Wales.

XXXVI.

He tired of Dudley's china and his pictures;
   Nor cared for Pender's most elaborate "feeds";
He wearied of those Chiswick Garden mixtures,
   Where names so heterogeneous one reads.
He shunned, at last, all Lady Devonshire's "fixtures,"
   And feared the Waldegravian "friendly leads."
And, as a child a powder or a pill dreads,
Shirked Art at Mr. Hope's and Lady Mildred's.

XXXVII.

The Hamiltonian Hall no more he seeks,
   Nor treads the corridors of Leveson Gower;
The *tableaux vivants* down at Mrs. Freke's
   Raise no excitement in him as of yore;
He did not go to Grosvenor House for weeks,
   And never darkened Bentinck's ducal door.
In fact, the more he saw, and heard, and knew,
Did *la crême de la crême* seem but "sky-blue."

XXXVIII.

And even intrigues grew great bores at last,
   For they, too, savoured strongly of De Brett;
And, also, when a girl was more than fast,
   Her sin was fenced about with etiquette
To such extent that Duan was aghast
   At an hypocrisy unequalled yet;
And longing for an unrestrain'd variety,
Vow'd he would have the sins *sans* the society.

XXXIX.

So he to the "ten thousand" bade adieu,
   And said "Good-bye" to "Prince's" and its rink—
("Prince's" is too select for most of you,
   But there are warmish corners there, we think),
And with regret he said "Farewell" to few
   Of those who'd given him their meat and drink:

For as the average modern dinner goes,
'Tis a fit torture not for friends but foes.

XL.

He also turned upon Mayfair his back,
   And wholly left Belgravia in the lurch;
Gladly he gave Tyburnia the "sack,"
   In vain did Kensingtonia for him search;
He sailed completely on another tack,
   And gave up leaving cards or going to church—
Sins of omission in the topmost zone,
Which no committed virtues can condone.

XLI.

So now behold Jon Duan set quite free
   To suck the sweets from every London flower;
More like a butterfly, perhaps, than bee—
   For he did not improve the shining hour.
And had you chance and money, then we'd see
   If you, good reader, would own virtue's power.
For though the truth, sweet innocents, may hurt you,
Necessity's a powerful aid to virtue.

XLII.

How often acrid women virtue boast,
   Of which a trial would be a new sensation!
So, all the goody-goody priggish host,
   Are prigs perforce—they follow their vocation.
It is no credit to a senseless post,
   Because it does not fall into temptation;
Nor do we crown an icicle with laurels
Because it hasn't thawn into soft morals.

XLIII.

Therefore, our hero we don't mean to censure
   For having, what in slang is called his "fling";
He had to bear the sequel of his venture,
   And Nature is the goddess that we sing!—
For he who breaks her laws, or tries to wrench her
   Rules, so well balanc'd, naturally will bring—
Sure as contempt has fallen on Bazaine—
Just retribution and deserved disdain.

XLIV.

This granted, without any more preamble,
   Duan may start upon his search for pleasure;
We'll try to only chronicle his scramble,
   And not to moralize in every measure;

But if again we into preaching ramble,
  And weary out your patience and your leisure,—
Why, blame the metre!—which, of all we know,
Most tempts one from the beaten track to go.

XLV.

The public pleasures of our wondrous city
  Are not so plentiful as one would think,
Thanks to the sapient licensing committee,
  Who from the very thought of dancing shrink.
The Alhambra's spoiled—it is a shame and pity;
  The Holborn's given up to meat and drink,
And nothing could be just now so forlorn
As passing a long evening at Cremorne!

XLVI.

'Twas not in this direction Duan found
  The pleasure that he sought. He went, 'tis true,
The usual dull and soul-depressing round,
  And raked and rioted till all was blue;
He trod, of course, the old familiar ground,
  And liked it not a whit more than did you,
When you—*consule Planco*—'woke with pain,
And cursed the women and the vile champagne.

XLVII.

He went to the Alhambra, found it dirty,
  With "Ichabod" writ large upon its walls.
He sought the "Duke's" about eleven thirty,
  And wandered listlessly through Argyle's Halls;
Saw Tottie, Lottie, Dottie, Mottie, Gertie,—
  And liquors stood responsive to their calls;
Thinking the openly conducted traffic
Was far more Cityish in its tone than Sapphic.

XLVIII.

He lounged about the Haymarket, and smoked;
  And felt quite sad amidst its scenes and sights;
He haunted bars, and with their Hebes joked,
  He "finished" at Kate H.'s, several nights;
He saw, God knows! a mass of misery, cloak'd
  With ghastly gaiety, beneath the lights,
Until the hideous visions made his soul burn,
And sent him virtuously back to Holborn.

XLIX.

For he had taken Chambers in Gray's Inn,
  Since he had cut the West End so completely,
And had a laundress smelling much of gin,
  Who could do nothing noiselessly or neatly.
'Twas here his other life he did begin,
  In rooms whose look-out, chosen most discreetly,
Show'd those old elms, each one of them a big tree,—
And here he sinned 'neath his own vine and fig-tree.

L.

If walls had ears!—the notion is not new—
  You'd like to hear Jon Duan's tell their tale.
And still, the same old notion to pursue,
  If chairs and sofas talked, we would avail
Us of their confidences, also; you
  May be quite sure that, were they writ, the sale
Of these poor rhymes, then, would be more immense,
Though hypocritic cries rose more intense.

LI.

As 'tis, we'd Figaro want to tabulate
  For us a list of all Jon Duan's loves;
To catalogue his *cartes*, each with its date,
  And give the history of the flowers and gloves,
And snipp'd-off tresses, which in numbers great
  From time to time into his drawer he shoves.
But, failing that, here is a peg to hang
A little song upon, that once he sang.

The Maid of Clapham.

1.

Maid of Clapham! ere I part,
Tell me if thou hast a heart!
For, so padded is thy breast,
I begin to doubt the rest!
Tell me now before I go—
Αῤ θοῦ ἀλλ μᾶδε υπόρνῶ?

2.

Are those tresses thickly twined,
Only hair-pinned on behind?
Is thy blush which roses mocks,
Bought at three-and-six per box?
Tell me, for I ask in woe—
Αῤ θοῦ ἀλλ μᾶδε υπόρνῶ?

3.

And those lips I seem to taste,
Are they pink with cherry-paste?
Gladly I'd the notion scout,
But do those white teeth take out?
Answer me, it is not so—
Ἀῤ ϑοῦ ἀλλ μᾶδε υπὀρνῶ?

4.

Maid ot Clapham! come, no larks!
For thy shoulders leave white marks—
Tell me! quickly tell to me
What is really real in thee!
Tell me, or at once I go—
Ἀῤ ϑοῦ ἀλλ μᾶδε υπὀρνῶ?

LII.

His taste for girls was certainly eclectic,
 He loved the dark ones even as the fair;
He liked complexions pale, complexions hectic,
 He liked black tresses, he liked golden hair,
And ne'er got amatorily dyspeptic—
 Which is a state of heart by no means rare;
But managed by the means detailed above,
To never be completely out of love.

LIII.

Gussie was dark, a perfect gipsy she,
 With sloe-black eyes, of raven hair an ocean;
With lips so red, they well might tempt the bee,
 And full of many a quaint artistic notion,—
She was an artist's model, you could see
 It was so in her graceful, flowing motion.
It must, we think, be a most pleasing duty
To draw and paint the curves of female beauty.

LIV.

The girl had sat for many a well-known painter,
 Before her path across Jon Duan's came;
As beggar-girl, as sinner, and as saint, her
 Pretty face oft peeped from out a frame.
In '73 no picture could be quainter
 Than that—it bore a rising painter's name—
Which represented her in grandma's bonnet—
We recollect that it called forth a sonnet.

LV.

Now Jon was no great artist, that was sure,—
 Not much he'd ever drawn but bills and cheques,
But to improve, he managed to secure
 This model's services—nor did it vex
Her, when, with face and voice alike demure,
 He called her the most lovely of her sex,
And pleading but poor skill to paint her beauty,
Yet many times a week essayed the duty.

LVI.

Nor did he weary of his occupation,
 For she was very jolly in her style;
Full of artistic chatter, animation
 In every look, and word, and frown, and smile.
And she could play—a great consideration
 To have a girl who thus your time can while;
And take a hand at whist, and play it, too—
A thing not one girl in ten-score can do.

LVII.

And naturally she was very skilful
 In falling into stock artistic poses;
A little petulant, sometimes, and wilful—
 Que voulez-vous? Without a thorn no rose is.
A "model" girl is very often still full
 Of that old Adam which the Church, you know, says
Is in us all; and which, as we're advised,
Means all our hearts are old (Mc) Adamized.

LVIII.

Be this as 't may. In time Miss Gussie went,
 And fair-haired Looie reigned in her stead;
Whilst Duan seemed by no means discontent—
 Having escaped the plate flung at his head
By the retiring beauty;—nor gave vent
 To vain regrets, nor wished that he were dead.
Instead of this, his spirits seemed to rally,
As he cried, "L'Art est mort, so, Vive le Ballet!"

LIX.

For Loo was in the ballet at the Strand,
 And thus possess'd that halo of romance
Which footlights ever throw on all who stand
 Before them, let them act, or sing, or dance.—
It even spreads a little o'er the band—
 Nay, we a weak-kneed fellow knew by chance,
Who was a very bad and drunken "super,"
'Cause his admirers treated him to "cooper."

LX.

Looie was in the foremost row, a token
　　She danced with more than average ability:
And many a stallite's heart no doubt she'd broken
　　With her plump legs and marvellous agility.
But when our hero once to her had spoken,
　　The intimacy grew with great facility.
And as he knew the critics, and had means,
Jon Duan spent much time behind the scenes,

LXI.

And waited for his charmer many nights,
　　And hung about what "Yanks" call the "theàter";
Supped to the full on Thespian delights;
　　But p'rhaps his feeling of delight was greater
When she rehearsed new dances in her tights,
　　He being her only critic and spectator.
Had he been good, he should have tried to stop her,
But, then, it is so nice to be improper.

LXII.

"Man's a phenomenon, one knows not what,
　　And wonderful beyond all wondrous measure:
'Tis pity, though, in this sublime world, that
　　Pleasure's a sin, and sometimes sin's a pleasure."
Which lines are Byron's. You will find them pat,
　　If you look up *Don Juan* when you've leisure.
If sin's unpleasant, as the churches din so,
Then, why the dickens is it that we sin so?

LXIII.

Is it unpleasant?—that's the awkward question—
　　And many sinners answer with a "No!"
Jon Duan, when he had no indigestion,
　　Thought it was most decidedly not so;
That if you pick your sins, and all the rest shun,
　　You may most pleasantly through this world go.
Which shows us plainly, 'spite his great vitality,
How very cold and dead was his morality.

LXIV.

How else could he have dared to thus defy
　　The ethics of society and Hymen;
And half a dozen amoratas try,
　　Just like as many tarts bought of a pieman,
And then dismiss them with a curt good-bye,
　　As though they'd been so many Brighton flymen?
No! if our hero had the right way fix'd on,
Then what becomes of married life at Brixton—

LXV.

At Peckham, Clapham, Islington, and Walworth,
　　At Ball's Pond, Pentonville, and Kentish Town?
Surely these homes of misery you'll call worth
　　The great rewards that virtue always crown.
Jon Duan's wicked life is naught at all worth,
　　And he and all like him must be put down.
He's happy, truly, but his joy's unstable—
Most married ones are always miserable.

LXVI.

Sewing-machines and cooks on trial we get,
　　And horses we may try before we buy;
And ev'n if afterwards we should regret
　　Our bargains, we can sometimes off them cry;—
But matrimonial bargains, don't forget,
　　Last till one of the parties chance to die.
'Twas knowing if he married, 'twas for life,
Made Duan hesitate to take a wife.

LXVII.

'Twas very wrong of him, of course, to do so:
　　Men ought from marriage never thus to shrink;
For is it not ordained?—Jon Duan knew so,
　　And yet stood lingering at the altar's brink.
He thought that he the life-long step might rue; so
　　Do others; and there are some men who think
Hannen would hear less charging and denial
If we could take our spouses upon trial.

LXVIII.

On trial, indeed! Why, not one in ten thousand
　　Women would e'er be wed on such a term;
For rare's the one who does not break her vows, and
　　Show very quickly that she has the germ
Of mutiny within her, and makes rows, and
　　Most speedily her husband's fears confirm.
If married life were terminable at will,
How many would next week be married still?

LXIX.

How long our young friend loved the ballet dancer
　　We do not mean to tell, nor shall we add

More details of his charmers; 'twould not answer
 To waste so much space on what is so bad.
No! let us shun the subject like a cancer,
 'Twould only make us and our readers sad.
We will, instead, with their permission, fit a
Small song in here—Jon sung it with his zither.

To Ethel.

1.

O, pocket edition of Phryne!
 Your robe is bewitchingly Greek;
O, kiss me, my charmer most tiny—
 I mean on my mouth, not my cheek.
Come, sit on my knee and be jolly—
 The classical's now out of date—
And let us toast passion and folly—
 For you are not marble, thank fate!

2.

What! haven't you heard of her story,
 And how all her judges she won,
By suddenly showing her glory
 Of beauty, which warmed like the sun?
Yes, that was in Cecrops' fair city,
 And we are 'neath London's green trees—
But, Tiny, you're awfully pretty,
 And I'll be your judge, if you please.

LXX.

Love is an ailment dangerously zymotic—
 'Twould be no use for us to here deplore
That Duan's song has savour so erotic—
 No! we will leave him on his second-floor,
Puffing the weed the doctors call narcotic,
 And with his eyes fixed keenly on his door—
Whom he expects it's not for us to say,
It *isn't* his old laundress, any way.

LXXI.

What are the Mission people all about,
 That to Gray's Inn they do not send a preacher?
Why to Ashanti and Fiji go out,
 And leave unvisited by tract or teacher
The district where the foolish fling and flaunt,
 And sink the Christian too much in the creature?
Call back! say we, the men from Timbuctoo,
There's better work at home for them to do.

LXXII.

We mean to start a Mission of our own,
    To preach the Testament in Grosvenor Square;
And when the funds sufficiently have grown,
    We'll send a Missionary to Mayfair;
And we'll leave large-type leaflets on the throne,
    And preach in Pall Mall in the open air :
In time, too, we'll endeavour to arrange
A set of sermons for the Stock Exchange.

LXXIII.

The texts used there shall be, "Thou shalt not
    steal,"
    And "Lying lips are an abomination"; *
All the discourses should most plainly deal
    With paper frauds and bubble speculation.
How sweet to make a cheating broker kneel
    In penitent and tearful agitation !
Surely one London broker on his knees
Is worth a score of Christianised Burmese.

LXXIV.

What could be grander than a "Bull" in tears,
    Or a "Bear" giving up all he possesses ?
How pleasant to the missionary's ears
    When some McEwen his dark deed confesses,
And promises repentance ! when the jeers
    Of jobbers cease ; and all the Mission presses
Spread the glad news that, as they're just advised,
Fifteen stockbrokers were last night baptized.

LXXV.

Oh ! what a noble work the news to spread
    Amongst the streets and alleys of the City ;
To tell the heathens there what has been said
    Of those who have no principle or pity :
To pour denunciation on their head,
    And wake up Lothbury with a pious ditty !
And oh ! how eagerly we yearn and pant
To send a special missionary to Grant !

LXXVI.

And this should be his message—" Albert ! thou
    Of whom 'tis said, ' He waxeth fat and kicketh,'

---

* These passages are evidently not included in the "Scripture" in use in Capel Court ; though we suppose it is generally known there that " Barabbas was a publisher." We have heard of the "Thieves' Litany," maybe there is such a volume in existence as the "Stockbrokers' Bible."

Let fear and trembling come upon thee now,
    For closer than a leech McDougal sticketh ;—
Let consternation sit upon thy brow
    When thought of ' Emma,' thy profuse heart
    pricketh, —
Nor glory in thy riches—house or arable—
But recollect the rich fool in the parable !"

LXXVII.

The " upper ten " there parlous state should see;
    There should be preaching at the Carlton Club ;
A Boanerges should the preacher be,
    With words and will Aristos' sin to drub.
And Lazarus should come from penury,
    And hold forth in the " Row," upon a tub.
Whilst some great light—the "toppest" of top-
    sawyers—
Should the New Testament proclaim to lawyers.

LXXVIII.

The publishers, too, must not be forgotten,
    Since great above all others is their need ;
For Paternoster Row is getting rotten,
    And worships but one God, and that is
    " Greed."
To lie, cheat, cozen, and to cringe and cotton,
    Is now the publisher's adopted creed ;
They're grasping, greedy, vulgar, and omni-
    vorous,—
From publishers, we pray, Good Lord deliver us !

LXXIX.

Our readers perhaps by this time will be ready,
    To pray to be delivered from us ;—
Our Pegasus, in fact, had got his head, he
    Often bites his bit, and bolts off thus.
But now we promise that his pace we'll steady,
    And, without any further fume or fuss,
To Duan we'll return, though, since we started,
He very likely has to bed departed.

LXXX.

There let us leave him—for 'tis doubtless best
    To "ring down" whilst we set the next new
    scene on—
Leaning, it may be, on a maiden's breast,—
    Happy the man's who's such a place to lean on !
For certain he's caressing or caress'd :—
    But it is two a.m.; and we have been on
Rhythmical duty since we dined at eight :
We'll put the light out—it is getting late.

Canto The Sixth.

I.

"AU Grand Hotel, Paris, the 10th November—
   Dear Boy,—The stage is going to the deuce,
The kiosques, naked, and there's not an ember
   Of fiery France alive. It is no use
To seek the Imperial Paris we remember,
   Dear Venus Meretrix of cities, loose
But lovely, and beloved—of Saxon tourists,
Who when abroad are not such rigid purists.

II.

"School atlases still tell us it's called Paris,
   They talk French still, a little, in its walls—
Though nasal North American less rare is;
   There still are *cafés*, and the naughty balls;
The Boulevards—though they're widowed of Gus Harris,
   Are not precisely hung with shrouds and palls;
Crowds, not more virtuous and not more solemn,
Still saunter past the new-erected Column.

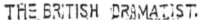

THE BRITISH DRAMATIST.

III.

"Still in the Palais Royal, yellow covers,
   Abhorred by strict mammas in England, beg
Attention to their tales of loves and lovers,
   Crammed full of wholesome nurture as an egg—
Still, at street crossings, prurient Saxon rovers
   Look shocked at some faint *soupçon* of a leg,
Disclosed by vicious sylph or luring *modiste*,
Loose-principled—but very tightly bodiced.

IV.

"But the sweet home of British drama—that is
   A thing to seek as Schliemann seeks for Troy—
Home of the Capouls, Schneiders, Faures, and Pattis,
   Who take our millions, and who give us joy—
The birthplace of all *personæ dramatis*
   That e'er amused since Taylor was a boy,
Where is it?—where's the generous Providence
Whence all of us draw plots, and fame, and pence?

V.

"Where's the great reservoir of milk and water
   Which Oxenford's keen pen was wont to tap,
Before that horrid Madame Angot's daughter
   Had made the pure old five-acts seem like pap?

Those old '*grandes machines*,' full of fire and
    slaughter,
  And doeskin boots, that soothed one's evening
    nap,
  Where are they?—Ah! they have left this drear
    and pallid day
  To Walter Scott, improved by Andrew Halliday.

VI.

"The Vaudeville, preposterous and broad,
  Where heroes in check suits could damn a bit,
  And into bed get, while the house guffawed—
  And those brave poker-scenes that made us
    split—
The singing chambermaids who weren't outlawed
  By chaste dress circles that like Gilbert's wit—
The gay old farce, loud, jovial, coarse, and fat—
Hasn't disastrous Sedan left us that?

VII.

"It hasn't, I assure you—not a line.
  I've tried the Variétés and Palais Royal,
  But though our H.R.H.'s tastes incline
    To that snug house—and though I'm strictly
      loyal—
  I can't find the old salt; defeats refine,
  And theatres here have grown so very coy all,
  They have not one poor smile for "adaptators"—
  Those eunuchs who all yearn to look like paters.

VIII.

"As poor Brooks said—'There's nothing in the
    papers,'
  And I remark there's nothing on the stage—
The old familiar bony legs cut capers,
  Their owners in the old intrigues engage
Before the usual crowd of languid gapers,
  Kept silent by the sanctity of age.
Lemaître and Bernhardt still pass round the hat,
Léonide's still lean, and Celine's still fat.

IX.

"And there you have the worst of the collapse
  Of our dear famous factory of plays.
Now, what is to be done? We're tired of traps,
  And care no more to see blue-fire ablaze
Around three-score old ladies, who want caps
  And snuff to comfort their declining days.
Poor Comedy, the Comedy of Sheridan,
Is done—and Mrs. Bancroft echoes: *Very* done.

X.

"The *Demi-monde* won't do: it *is* enticing,
  I own—but no; it really will not do,
E'en though we made it seemlier by splicing
  A *roué* and a courtezan or two,
According to the English way of icing
  French fancies, found red-hot and deemed too
    true;
And even then, when we have changed the visors,
There's always that prude Piggott with the scissors.

XI.

"Always those scissors! Halévy might yield
  A thing or two, and Meilhac's not quite dried;
But what can a poor devil do when sealed
  To that old haggard Spiritual bride,
The Censorship? Its maimed limbs scarcely healed,
  On to the stage your poor piece takes a stride,
And halts half-way, then with a limp crawls out—
For those official shears are worse than gout.

XII.

"I think we must encourage 'native talent'—
  That's how we'll make our poverty seem grand,
And not at all enforced by the repellant
  Airs of our French originals. Your hand
Put into those deep drawers, where all the gallant
  And unplayed amateurs, a numerous band,
Have left the ashes of their simple hopes—
Those MSS. that no one ever opes.

XIII.

"Perhaps you'll find a pearl of rarest price,
  Or rubbish written by a lord, which will
Do quite as well; the public aren't too nice
  When a peer condescends to hold a quill.
Give it to Byron—he'll put in the spice.
  But as for here—my verdict still is: *nil!*
There's not a piece to steal, so we must do one
Ourselves. Ta, ta, old boy; *tibi*—Jon Duan."

XIV.

One doesn't always call a manager
  Old boy, or write as lengthily as this.
Some, one should call "My Lord," *one* "Reverend
    Sir,"
And many a "Mrs." more correctly "Miss!"
But fame, thank Heaven, 's a glorious leveller,
  And straight inducts you into that great bliss
Of penetrating the most awful portals,
And treating even managers as mortals.

SAMPSON & CO.,

SHIRT TAILORS.

SOLE MAKERS OF THE

SURPLICE SHIRT.

INDIAN SHIRTS,
7s. 6d. to 10s. 6d.

Made from a soft longcloth, and suitable for India wear.

LONGCLOTH SHIRTS, Military Fronts,
5s. 6d. to 6s. 6d.

Orders from Abroad carefully executed.

India Flannel Shirts, 10s. 6d. to 14s. 6d.	Saratta Gauze Cotton Shirts, 8s. 6d. 9s. 6d.
Cashmere or Silk, 16s. 6d. to 18s. 6d.	Dress Shirts, Night Shirts,
Best French Printed, 8s. 6d. to 9s. 6d.	Front Studs, Links, Collar Studs, &c.

SAMPSON AND CO. invite special attention to their SURPLICE SHIRTS, as being peculiarly adapted in their shape for India. Outfit orders can be executed at the shortest notice, as all Shirts and Collars are made on their own premises. Gentlemen returning from India would find a large and well assorted Stock to select from. Great attention is bestowed upon the Shrinking of Flannels.

'A REGISTER KEPT OF ALL SHIRTS MADE TO MEASURE.

Detailed Outfit List and Self-measurement Cards sent on Application.

India Gauze Vests and Drawers.	Rugs, Plaids, Austrian Blankets.
Fine Merino and Cotton Half-Hose.	Waterproof Goods, Ground Sheets.
Fine Pure Woollen Hosiery.	Regulation Overland Trunks, Cabin Bags.

TAILORING DEPARTMENT.

Coloured or White Flannel Suits, 45s. to 55s.	Patrol Jackets, 25s. to 45s.
India Tweed Suits, 55s. to 75s.	Dress Suits. Frock or Morning Coats.
Brown Holland or Drill Suits, 35s. to 55s.	Dressing Robes. Lounge Suits.
White Drill Trousers, 13s. 6d. to 18s. 6d.	Overcoats. Riding Belt Drawers.

GLOVES SEWN WITH THREAD FOR INDIA WEAR.

SAMPSON & CO., India and Colonial Outfitters,
130, OXFORD STREET, Near Holles Street, London, W.

TO THE READERS OF JON DUAN.

We reprint from The Times, *of Nov. 26th, the Report re* WARD *v.* BEETON, *in order that the purchasers and readers of* JON DUAN *may have a correct version of the question raised between* Mr. BEETON *and his Publishers. We should no trepeat this notice were it not for the rumours which have been freely circulated that* JON DUAN *would not be published. Even coercion has been used to prevent certain tradesmen lending us their valuable assistance in the production of the New Annual.*

The Public and the Trade are now in the position of being our judges, and we shall rest satisfied with the verdict which may be accorded us.

From "The Times," Nov. 26, 1874.

Before Vice-Chancellor Sir R. MALINS.)

WARD *v.* BEETON ("BEETON'S CHRISTMAS ANNUAL").

THIS was a motion on behalf of the plaintiffs, Messrs. Ward and Lock, the publishers, for an injunction to restrain the defendant, Mr. S. O. Beeton, from publishing or circulating any advertisements or letters representing that he was interested or concerned in any annual book or publication other than "Beeton's Christmas Annual," published by the plaintiffs, or that the defendant's connexion with the plaintiffs' firm was terminated, or that the use of the defendant's name by the plaintiffs for the purposes of their "Beeton's Christmas Annual" was improper or unauthorized. According to the statements contained in the bill, the defendant was in business on his own account as a publisher down to the year 1866, and among the publications of which he was the proprietor was "Beeton's Christmas Annual," now in its 15th year. In 1866 the plaintiffs purchased the copyrights and business property of the defendant, and in September of that year an agreement was entered into between the plaintiffs and the defendant, by which it was provided, among other things, that the defendant was to devote himself to the development of the plaintiffs' business and not to be interested in any other business without their consent; that the plaintiffs were to have the use of the defendant's name for the purposes of their present and future publications, and that the defendant should not permit the use of his name for any other publication without their consent; and the defendant was to be remunerated by a salary which was at first to consist of a fixed annual sum, and was subsequently to be equivalent to a fourth share of the profits of the plaintiffs' business. Under this agreement "Beeton's Christmas Annual" was published by the plaintiffs with the assistance of the defendant down to and including Christmas last. In the year 1872 the annual consisted of a production called "The Coming K——." It was published, however, as the plaintiffs alleged, without their having seen the MSS., and, as it contained passages which they considered were open to grave objections, they refused to print or publish a second edition of it. In 1873 the annual consisted of a publication called "The Siliad," which was written by the same authors as "The Coming K——." In July last the plaintiffs applied to the defendant to prepare the volume of the annual for Christmas next, but desired that its character and contents might differ from those of "The Siliad," with which they were dissatisfied ; the defendant, however, "neglected to prepare or assist in preparing the same." In October last the plaintiffs heard that the defendant was engaged in preparing another annual in opposition to theirs. A correspondence ensued, in which the plaintiffs gave the defendant notice that they would maintain their rights, and required him to make proper arrangements for the production of the annual, while the defendant denied that he was in fault, and alleged that the plaintiffs had rejected the production he had proposed, which was to be by the authors of "The Coming K——," and that those gentlemen had then made their own arrangements for publishing their work. The plaintiffs then made arrangements with the authors of "The Siliad" for the annual of 1874, and announced it by advertisements in the newspapers, under the title of "Beeton's Christmas Annual for 1874, 15th season." The title of the coming annual is "The Fijiad." The defendant then caused advertisements to be inserted in the *Standard, Athenæum,* and other newspapers, addressed to booksellers, advertisers, and the public, stating that he had no hand in the annual announced by the plaintiffs; that he devised long ago his usual annual in collaboration with the authors of "The Coming K——" and "The Siliad ;" that the title of the annual now in the press was "Jon Duan;" that it was written by the authors of "The Coming K——," and "The Siliad," and would not be published by the plaintiffs, but by another publisher. Under these circumstances the present bill was filed yesterday, and in pursuance of leave then obtained the motion for injunction was made this morning. The defendant did not appear ; and upon an affidavit that service of the notice of motion had been effected upon him before five o'clock yesterday afternoon at his country residence, an order was made by the Court for an injunction in terms of the motion, extending *until the hearing of the cause.*

London : WELDON & CO., 15, Wine Office Court, Fleet Street.

Hard Facts.—"Gone to the Wall."

XV.

The person whom Jon Duan thus addressed
    Had an odd mania—general with his class—
For novelties, without which Spring's no zest
    In managerial eyes: he'd fix his glass,
Perceive the world with April-green new-dressed,
    And only think: the Spring's turned up the gas,
We've done Burnand—for fear of a reversal,
It's time to put Bob Reece into rehearsal.

XVI.

He'd got Jon Duan this year—a rare catch,
    That bothered Buckstone sorely, and made Bateman
Talk privately of bowie-knives; a batch
    Of critics—his club-fellows—all elate, man
The yards of paper barks, where they keep watch
    On actors, ready to call Irving great man,
And Neville, stick;—or quite the other way:
It just depends on what their rivals say.

XVII.

Hollingshead hides his head; the craft looks sour,
    From classic Surrey to coquettish Court.
It's such a glorious thing to get the flower
    Of a young author's mind, whom wide report
Proclaims the sovereign genius of the hour,
    And when the stale Byronic stream runs short—
Which even that perpetual fountain may,
When Gilbert's proper, and "Old Sailors" pay.

XVIII.

You managers, when wearied—as you weary
    The public—of the tight dramatic ring
That writes eulogious notices, and dreary
    Dramas, alternately, from Spring to Spring,
Don't dare too much—and don't revive Dundreary,
    But simply ask a man whom critics sing,
And at whose feet the publishers all grovel,
To dialogue you his last prurient novel.

XIX.

There is your man. He's been well advertised,
    Which saves a lot of posting and of puffs;
You know the papers where his copy's prized,
    And which, therefore, are sure not to be rough
On his new venture. Then a book, disguised
    In five acts, with a new name's just the stuff
To run two hundred nights; we all adore
Hearing the jokes we've read a month before.

XX.

But, following the ancient pure tradition
    Of English art to borrow from the French,
Jon Duan had set out upon a mission,
    To see what Paris drama one could wrench
Into a Saxon shape, by clever scission
    Of evil branches, which emit a stench
We breathe with rapture at the "Delass. Com.,"
But call a pestilential death at home.

XXI.

And seeing there was nothing that could give
    The Insular adapter a fair chance
To catch the rare French nectar in a sieve—
    For that's the way we get our sustenance,
Who don't know French, go to the play—and live!—
    Jon Duan shook the sterile dust of France
From off his feet, and reappeared in town,
Resolved to bring out three acts of his own.

XXII.

Then in a dim and dusty room, somewhere
    Near Covent Garden, a dull chamber, smelling
Of orange-peel and gas, the native air
    Of Thespis, there ensued long talk, which dwelling
On things theatrical, would make the hair
    Of stage-struck youths stand upright—so repelling,
Hard and materialistic as a Hun's,
The manager who's looking for long "runs."

XXIII.

"I have told you so: I'd much prefer a *bouffe*,
    A *bouffe* of thorough native growth: d'you see?
Something that we can say affords a proof
    Wit and song ain't a French monopoly.
Something that shows at times the cloven hoof—
    Of Meilhac, great in impropriety,
But sentimental chiefly—even sad,
A Tennysonian pastoral gone mad.

XXIV.

"There'd be a part for Cecil—heavy father,
    Eccentric, muddle-headed: that's his line.
We must give little Lou a lift—I'm rather
    Spoony on little Lou; besides, she'll shine,
If you but give her a catch-song to gather
    The plaudits of the gods with. *There's* a mine
Worth working—there's ten thousand pounds in that—
And, by-the-by, give Isabel some fat.

XXV.

" Lord D—— insists upon it : Bella must
    Have three good scenes, at least, in which to drop
Her h's—or the old boy will entrust
    His love and money to a rival shop.
There's Belamour, too, who will not be thrust
    Into a minor part ; he'll want a sop,
Because of those fine legs of his, on which
He counts to catch a "relict" old and rich.

XXVI.

"As for the rest, we'll have a galaxy
    Of stars seduced by gold from lesser spheres :
Cox, Terry, Toole, Brough, and the rest ; you'll see
    We'll do the thing superbly—— Now, my dears !"
(This to two pleasing damsels who'd made free
    To push the door ajar, and stood all ears,
And those all red, regarding the uncertain
And ghostly region called Behind the Curtain.)

XXVII.

The postulants, for such they were, of course,
    Were average growths of English womanhood,
Sprung from the same poor petty tradesman source,
    Not capable of much ill or much good ;
But conscious of some appetite perforce
    Restrained, the which in their weak natures stood
For mind, ambition, heart—some simple needs
Of love, champagne, fine dresses, and good feeds.

XXVIII.

We all know, though decorum keeps us mute,
    How shop-girl, servant wench, and seamstress
    feel,
When pretty broughams of world-wide repute
    Bear sinning sisters by on rapid wheel,
And Regent Street's battalions, in pursuit
    Of night-bound swell, flash by them, down at heel
And threadbare, thinking—not : how shocking !—
    oh no—
But simply of their labouring lives : *Cui bono ?*

XXIX.

Cui bono, having learnt one's catechism
    And making shirts for close on ninepence each ?
Cui bono, all this vulgar heroism
    That only serves to make a parson preach
About our pure examples ? Egotism,
    That's what you pay—the moral that you teach ;
Vice has its brougham, Virtue its foul alley—
This is the reason why girls join the Ballet.

XXX.

The first one of the two who spoke had passed
   The Rubicon, and left false shame behind her ;
Her bonnet might have been a whit less fast,
   Her speech a bit more modest and refined ; her
Red hands bulged from Jouvin's gloves. She cast
   A side-leer at Jon Duan rather kinder
Than their acquaintance warranted, and said
   She knew the business ; she'd already played.

XXXI.

"At the East End Imperial Bower of Song,
   I used to sing 'The Chick-a-Leary Bloke,'
With breakdown, all complete. 'Twas rather strong—
   The beaks refused the licence. But I've spoke
To —— (here she whispered earnestly and long)
   He'll come down handsomely : just one small joke,
And then a dance. What! fifty pounds!—Well, then,
   You'll throw a speech in for another ten."

XXXII.

"It's sixty pounds; no salary at first."
   And then the manager turned round: "And you?"
The second humble applicant was cursed
   With knowledge of her own defects, and drew
Back as he spoke. Then feebly from her burst:
   "I heard you wanted figurantes who knew
Something of music, prepossessing—Oh,
   I want to know, sir, if I'm like to do !"

XXXIII.

Jon Duan pitied ; but his friend looked stern.
   This one had no Protector and no past.
She couldn't pay, and might expect to earn
   Her living—the pretension of her caste,
Who in each yawning trap and slide discern
   Mines where all women's treasures are amassed—
Diamonds, Bond Street dresses, silks and sashes,
   And tall Nonentities with blond moustaches.

XXXIV.

"Young woman, you may do ; I don't object
   To trying you : just bring your 'props' next week——"
"Props?"——"That's your shoes and tights; but recollect,
   You're never likely to do more than speak
Ten words, and show—your ankles. We expect
   Our ladies to wear costumes new and *chic*,
Which they provide—with some gems of pure water——
   The salary? It's five pounds ten per quarter.

XXXV.

"You couldn't live on that? Of course you can't.
   Did you expect it?—*Where* have you been taught?—
A brougham's at the door : its occupant
   Gets one pound ten a week—and she's just bought
A pair of bays—which proves she's not in want.
   No, no, young woman, salaries are nought—
Our treasurer don't count ; you'll find far finer—
   A millionaire—a dotard—or a minor.

XXXVI.

"All of them do it : it's the modern plan
   Of getting up a pretty ballet cheap ;
And since the public don't like Sheridan—
   Except as Amy—and since we can't keep
Ladies—most of them of enormous space—
   In silken robes and satin shoes; we leap
At amateurs with *protégées*, whose rage
   It is to see their darlings on the stage."

XXXVII.

Then they went back to business, and talked over
   Which points Odell should make, which speeches Stoyle ;
If Wyndham or Lal. Brough should do the lover,
   Say with Laverne or Farren as a foil.
And whether Miss A.'s part was not above her,
   Or Miss B. meet Miss C. without a broil.—
In short, the heavy talk, the prime First Cause
   Of plays received with rapturous applause.

XXXVIII.

Jon Duan gave in to the *bouffe* idea,
   His hopes resigning of regenerating
The public taste. He gazed, and could but see a
   Vast Amphitheatre, its lungs inflating
With one loud universal *Ave Dea*,
   Madonna Cascade of our own creating,
Gross, gaudy goddess of our fleshly charlatan
   Period, with tinsel wings and robes of tarlatan.

XXXIX.

That is the cry, the Ideal—— Oh, Rare Ben,
   See what they've made of your old jovial muse !

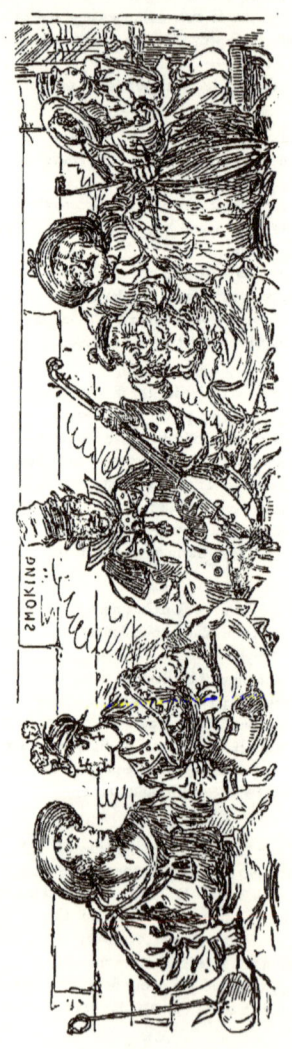

Enter, great Shade, no matter where or when,
   The bill of fare's the same—you cannot choose.
It's an Aquarium—and once again
   Fifty familiar naked backs one views—
Then naked breasts, legs, naked arms with wings
Of gauze—innumerable naked things !

XL.

The footlights glow on thin arms, twisted knees,
   Lean shoulders rising, fleshy chins that drop ;
Oh for the awful busts' concavities !
   Oh for the busts that don't know where to stop.
They smirk, and grin, and ogle at their ease,
   But one thinks vaguely of a butcher's shop
Lit up on Saturdays—one hears the cry,
A cry they all might echo : " Come, buy, buy !"

XLI.

Ah, one divines how, mute, the song-nymphs flee,
   And Watteau's muse drops down the magic brush
Before that swollen, restless, muddy sea
   Of shapeless flesh, pink with a painted blush ;
Those meagre shoulder-blades that don't agree,
   Those overflowing waists that corsets crush,
Those poor old calves, for twice a hundred nights
Entombed with pain in cherry-coloured tights.

XLII.

A sprite, long, lean, and languid as a worm,
   A sprite that trails a cotton-velvet cloak,
Carols a topic song, with not a germ
   Of tune or sense in it. Ay, Ben, they croak—
These mounds of chignons-false and flesh-infirm—
   Dreary distortions of thy Attic joke,
With tripping feet and leering eyes, and shifty,
As if they weren't all grandmammas of fifty !

XLIII.

Oh Byron, Farnie, oh Burnand, and Reece,
   Maybe your consciences are very full,
For you've committed many a dreary piece ;
   But oh, we'd hold your grievous sinnings null
If you had not—Heaven send your souls release !—
   You—and some thousand bales of cotton-wool—
Produced, to torture your long-suffering patrons,
That bevy of obese and padded matrons !

XLIV.

But Goldie, Cibber, Knowles, whene'er we pray
   For one gleam of your wit or poesy ;
When with the jingle of Lecocq, and bray
   Of Offenbach distraught, we make a plea

For Tobin or for Coleman—for the gay
　Old glorious peal of laughter, frank and free—
Bah ! cry the lessees—Helicon !—a treat !—
Sir—what the public dotes upon is Meat !

XLV.

And faith, they get it, calves and necks, huge
　　boulders
Smeared with cold-cream, and bismuth, and
　　ceruse;
Not much heart anywhere, but such fine shoulders !
　Not much art, but such bright metallic hues !
Fat Aphrodites—born for their beholders
　From froth of champagne-cup—upon their cruise
To spoil our gilded youth, dupe hoary age,
Making a bagnio of the British stage.

XLVI.

Jon Duan passed some agonizing weeks,
　Conning Joe Miller and his *Lemprière*;
Laying the strata of burlesque in streaks
　Of slang and puns ; also refusing fair
Touters for parts, with badly painted cheeks,
　And insolently red and oily hair;
Who pet one—till you don't know where to get to—
That is the worst of writing a libretto.

XLVII.

The paragraph, which, to the *Era* carried,
　The world tells that you're "on" a *bouffe*,
　　wakes up
Three hundred ladies, who have found life arid,
　Because they never dine, and seldom sup,
And who begin to pester you : if married,
　With gall they fill your matrimonial cup ;
If single—well, of course they will not hurt you—
Only their friendship don't conduce to virtue !

XLVIII.

As for the writing—that's the easiest part—
　So easy, that if it the public guessed,
They'd never pay to see Burnand, but start
　A theatre themselves—perhaps the best.
A plot—who listens ?—Dialogue—it's smart
　If loose ; for ladies, have them much undressed,
Have two French mimics, lime-light, vulgar jokes,
Danseuses like Sara, villains like Fred Vokes.

XLIX.

The formula's quite simple : all depends
　On an anachronism, the more absurd
The better. Take a monarch and his friends
　From Livy—Roman—for they're much preferred,
The Grecian's quite used up except for bends—
　Send them to Prince's, and pretend they've heard
Of Gladstone's pamphlets, Arnim's case, whatever
You choose, provided that you're not too clever.

L.

Talent will kill. Leave actors to invent
　Whatever gags they can ; they'll find a number,
Not too refined, about each day's event,
　At those dramatic "publics" which encumber
The lanes of Covent Garden. If they're spent,
　And find the audience somewhat prone to
　　slumber,
A wink, grimace, a slang phrase—clownish acting—
That stirs your patrons up—they're not exacting.

LI.

They have broad backs, and not too lively brains ;
　They'll bear whatever burdens you impose ;
So that the playbill says it entertains,
　Don't think of them—they'll never hiss nor doze,
Provided you leave room for Hervé's strains,
　And give them a perspective of pink hose
From back to footlights, in bright buoyant
　　masses—
Before six hundred levelled opera-glasses.

LII.

Jon Duan at his writing-table, strewn
　With delicately scented little notes—
All begging him, as a tremendous boon,
　To lengthen parts and shorten petticoats—
Wrote feverishly; and, humming o'er a tune,
　Beside him lounged his partner—who devotes
His life to writing can-can and fandango—
Waiting for *his* hour and *his* Madame Angot.

LIII.

" I must have that new song to-morrow—that
　About the second-class—four lines of six,
And two of four for chorus. You've been flat
　Of late ; redeem yourself this time, and mix
The Old Hundredth up with Hervé's pit-a-pat,
　Or any other of their Paris tricks."
The maëstro grumbled—then, remembering
Gluck's works at home—said he had just the thing.

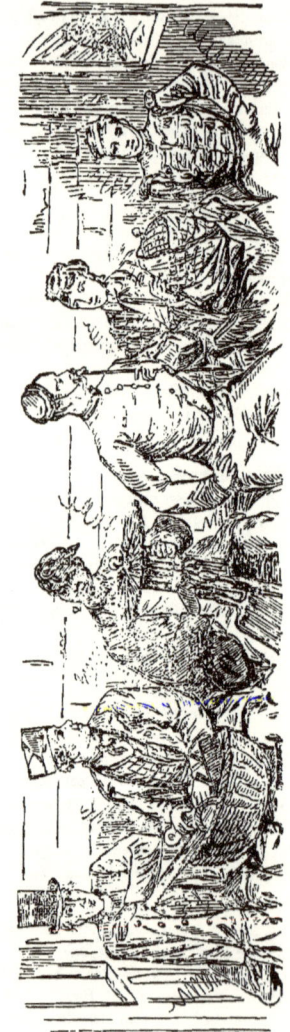

LIV.

"Have you heard anything from Piggott?" said he,
   After a pause, in which Jon Duan's quill
Ran fiercely. "I'm afraid our chance is shady,
   Unless you drop those jokes he's taken ill."
Just then the servant came, and said a lady
   Wanted Jon Duan, and the maëstro, still
Humming, went, leaving the field free to fair
Miss Constance Smith—Fitz-Fulke by *nom de
   guerre*.

LV.

The sweetest little creature man has ever
   Paid *modiste's* bills for; clouds of breezy curls
Blowing about her face, from such a clever
   And daring poem of a hat. She furls
Her veil, and, drugging one—and spreading fever—
   Fever of love and longing, round her whirls
A wind of subtle scents, corrupt and vicious—
Monstrous—exaggerated—and delicious!

LVI.

Wine-scarlet was her mouth—a flower of blood—
   A flower fed by the dew of many kisses;
And her eyes, fathomless, made one's heart thud,
   Though nought lay in their violet-grey abysses;
She was a creature, on the whole, who could
   Give man a vast variety of blisses—
The bliss of wooing, quarrelling, and playing—
With one monotonous—the bliss of paying!

LVII.

And yet she doesn't merit *all* the stones
   Austere and portly ladies, who "sit under"
Good parsons, are prepared to fling: she owns
   Some fervent, heavenly impulses, that sunder
Those venal lips, and break out in meek moans,
   Not less sincere than Pharisaic thunder,
About her sinfulness—whence fall, at times,
Prayers not less pure because they follow rhymes.

LVIII.

It is a little bosom full of eddies
   And counter-eddies, gusts, and whirls of whims,
That turn, re-turn her, till her pretty head is
   A chaos of conflicting thoughts, and swims,
A labyrinth through which no man can thread his
   Way—for she shifts and turns, and tacks and
     trims
So wildly, that Jon Duan's lighter, gayer
Poem—composed much later—must portray her.

Saint Célimène.

1

I'd give—the bliss she's given me—to perceive
   What moves her most—Caprice or Charity.
   Turn her glove back—just where it meets the
      sleeve—
   You smell involved incense, and patchouli.

2.

The march of music up long aisles, the dirges,
   Ormolu censers, waxen saints and lights,
Move the frail facile heart, albeit she merges
   Devoutest days in Saturnalian nights.

3.

I'd have you watch her as she bends alone
   In some prim pew, her mouth composed, hands
      crossed—
Fancying, vaguely, the priest's monotone
   Is something like Faure's lower notes in Faust.

4

She seeks salvation with the beautiful,
   Loves David's psalms—no less than Swinburne's
      sonnets—
Respects the *Follet* like a papal bull,
   And holds we're saved by perfect faith—and
      bonnets.

5.

Her mode of charity includes a ball ;
   And such her pity of each pauper claimant—
Watching her waltz, one deems she's given all—
   Even like St. Martin—more than half her rai-
      ment.

6.

When she comes begging for a fund or mission,
   Jew, Greek, Voltairian, weak or very wise,
You give your obolus—with shamed contrition,
   When Heaven returns it threefold through her
      eyes.

7.

And when you've watched Saint Célimène receding,
   Veiled like a Quakeress in coif of grey,
The recollection of her tender pleading
   Makes you admire Lord Ripon, for the day.

8.

Nor that same evening, when she quits the cloister,
   Is the antithesis of her bare breast
Aught than a drop of acid with one's oyster—
   The peppery pod that gives the dish a zest.

9.

For though one lose the fabled fox's quiet
   When the good grapes to low lips' level fall ;
She seems more fit for mankind's daily diet—
   "And she might like one really, after all."

10.

Like one ! to her guitar's erotic thrum
   She sets the preacher's precept : love all men ;
And founds her plea for pardon on *multum*—
   Et multos—amavi—like Magdalen.

11.

She makes a dainty mouth of doubt ; her fan
   Rebukes that soft Parisian purr : *Je t'aime !*
But she loves you—well, even as she can—
   A month or two—and then forgets your name.

12.

Forgets it all—till one day when her vapours
   Dispose to prayer the two months' devotee,
And in the glow of Ritualistic tapers,
   She finds a love not in her breviary.

LIX.

Aye, she was Molière's heroine, the jade !—
   "I am Miss Constance Fitzfulke." Duan bowed.
" They call me Rattlesnake." "Who's they ?" he
      said ;
And felt, somehow, girls should not be allowed
To make eyes of the enticing kind she made.
   "They ?—Why the fellows—all of them—a
      crowd,
De Lacy, Pierpoint, Charlie Lisle—you know,"
" I understand—you're not what one calls—slow !"

LX.

" Slow—not a bit, I'm fast as an express—
   Upon the Midland—and as dangerous.
One of those dolls all you men die to dress,
   So that your wives may safely copy us ;
You've got a part for me—now come, confess—
   You have one : something nice and frivolous,
None of your high art that thins all the houses
Of managers with tragic girls and spouses.

LXI.

"You'll hear me sing ; you'll see me dance : I
      flatter
Myself in both I'll rather startle you.
You see we vagabond ne'er-do-wells scatter
   The old traditions to the winds. We're new,

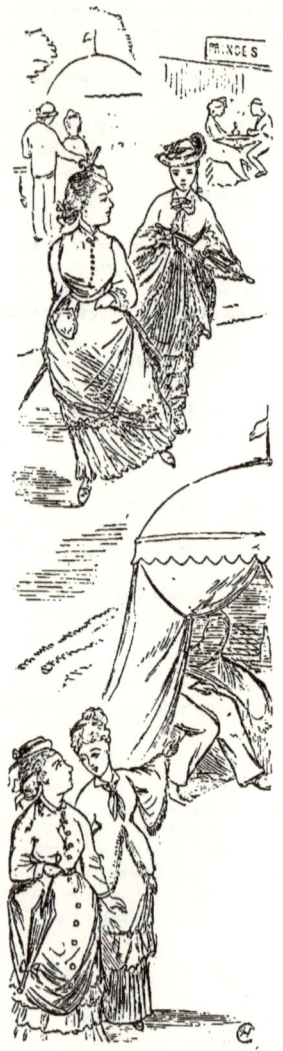

And young, and—well, not hideous." Staring at her,
Jon Duan, with conviction murmured : " True.'
" *We* 've seen life off the stage; while your old shoppy
Damsels know nought beyond a prompter's copy.

LXII.

" Our boudoirs, which are little Royal Exchanges,
   Afford a curious study of mankind ;
Roam as you like, from Tiber to the Ganges,
   And not a better point of sight you'll find.
But the pure player's vision seldom ranges
   Beyond—say that small spy-hole in the blind,
Through which *we* peer to see if *he* is in
His stall ; if 'paper' 's in the house—or 'tin.'

LXIII.

"Therefore my play will be original,
   I'll be myself upon the boards—a thing
The critic always sees—and ever shall,
   Till players are cultivated, and don't spring,
Like lichens, from the vestiges of all
   Professions they have failed in ; covering
Gown, surplice, red coat that's grown limp and dangles,
With tragic robes or acrobatic spangles."

LXIV.

Oh, wiser than the serpent—and much harder
   Than any stone, becomes the lovely woman
Who looks on London streets as a vast larder—
   A Hounslow Heath where she can stop and do man
Out of his purse and life. Good fortunes guard her,
   As though the one dear creature, frankly human,
In our sick century, whose jaundiced face is
Veiled, and who sespeech one endless periphrase is.

LXV.

Is 't vile—the *Demi monde?*—Why, sale and barter
   In noble drawing-rooms, are just the same,—
The *dot*, the face, the hoary lecher's garter,
   The father's money, and the mother's shame.
Let *trousseaux* rain, let diamonds of pure water
   Deck the dear well-bred maid who's made her game !—
Arrange for monsieur's mistress, madame's carriage—
You parody a vile Haymarket marriage.

LXVI.
The wicked Demi monde!—well, is your *monde*
  So whole and sound and healthy? Are your
     wives
Much better than "the others," and less fond
  Of princes, lions, lead they purer lives?
And is the Social Evil far beyond
  Your pinchbeck imitation? If it thrives,
Is it because it's honester and franker,
And don't put so much cold cream on the canker?

LXVII.
We never held Jon Duan an example
  Of virtue, such as one finds in the Peerage—
Which teems, of course, with many a brilliant
     sample
  Of godliness—above all in the sere age,
When man's ability to sin aint ample—
  But lots of genteel Josephs will, I fear, rage
(And wish they'd had a chance with the "be-
     guil-ah",)
On hearing how he gave in to Dalilah.

LXVIII.
He fell; where is the man who never fell
  At beck of like fair fingers, at th' invite
Of such a Syren, such a Satan's belle?—
  He'd be indeed a pure Arthurian knight,
Unlike the Marlborough Club men in Pall Mall.
  Jon Duan perished—we may'nt think him right,
Though even blood and iron do give in
To beauty decked out with the Wage of Sin——

LXIX.
Which isn't a bad salary on the whole,
  As wages go in these degenerate days;
When violet powder is less dear than coal;—
  At least we know that several pairs of bays
Are kept on those same wages, which a shoal
  Of Jew promoters, bankers, lordlings, pays,
Without reflecting on that heinous libel
About the Wage, they might find in the Bible.

LXX.
Jon Duan, fascinated, just declared
  The giving of a lady's part depended
Upon Miss Constance Fitzfulke—and he stared
  Quite rudely at the opulent and splendid figure
Before him. But, by no means scared,
  With coquetry and prudence subtly blended,
She said his demonstrations touched her heart—
But she would rather like to know her part.

LXXI.
"Your part, my princess? Oh, it is the best
  That even Rachel ever undertook.
The scene: Green Woods, that would make
     Telbin's breast
  Grow hot with envy, a small shady nook
That doesn't smell of paint—*The Prettiest
     Woman in the World, A Man*, whose look
Indicates spooniness beyond disguises—
Discovered talking as the curtain rises.

LXXII.
"The dialogue's poetic nonsense, Wills
  Would give his ears to equal; the bye-play
Is charming; not all Robertson's best quills
  Could sketch out 'business' half as sweet
     and gay:
The kisses are on flesh and blood that thrills—
  Not the light, cold contact of *Eau des Fées*,
With the best rouge, laid on by feet of hares,
To hide—the feet of crows from searching stares.

LXXIII.
"The Time—the Present. Costume—rich enough
  To show the wearers are of decent station,
And have a little leisure left for love.
  The Plot—ah, 'tis the airiest creation
That ever bard—strong-voiced or silent—wove;
  The simple plot that's pleased each age and
     nation
From Adam's day to Darwin's, though the latter,
Thanks unto Gilbert, finds the story flatter.

LXXIV.
"The Piece is Love—The Plot, it is love-making.
  It's had a run of some six thousand years.
Come, let us put it in rehearsal, taking
  The stage alone, and keeping it. Our ears
Weren't made for prompter's whispers!" But
     she, shaking
That sunny head of hers, said she had fears
About her memory—was he sure that *he'd* do?—
And was that quite a good *lever de rideau?*

LXXV.
It might come afterwards—as final farce,
  For farce it must be—she's nought, if not funny;
But a too quick *dénouement* often mars
  An author's best piece—and, above all, one he
Has planned so hastily. Profits are sparse,
  When one commences with so little money.
She'd see—a little later on—and her
Eyes said that day he'd be the Manager!

LXXVI.

"Well, though we're very full, I think I've found
  A small part, that will fit you like a glove,
In my 'Æneas,' a burlesque that's bound
  To beat 'Ixion.'" "You're a perfect love!—
But what's the dress?" "Oh, Roman robes."
  She frowned.
  "'Robes,' that sounds bad. Don't Roman
    swells approve
Of tights?" "Well, don't obey us to the letter,
Wear what you like—perhaps the less the better.

LXXVII.

"We've got Eumidia Johnson to play Dido.
  You'll have a scene with her."—"A scene with
    Miss
Eumidia Johnson!"—and Miss Constance cried:
  "Oh,
  You are a darling—Come now—there's a
    kiss!"—
"She enters speaking to a village guide, who
  Stays in the wings—Then Dido utters this:
'Is this the road to Sicily?'   The wight
Responds: 'Just past the cabstand, to your right.'

LXXVIII.

"You'll play the village lass."—"Well, what
    comes next?"
"Next—why there's nothing." "What! I
    don't appear
At all!"—and Miss Fitzfulke looked rather
    vexed,—
"Of course not." "Then why do you make
    me wear
A costume?"—The librettist said the text
Of his engagement stipulated there
Should be, in smallest details, a sublime
Aud true historic picture of the time.

LXXIX.

"Besides, you're sure to make Eumidia furious,
  She hates a pretty colleague worse than sin;
And then the Stalls are sure to be most curious
  To know who's Miss Fitzfulke, who ne'er
    comes in;—
A mystery is not at all injurious
  When figurantes, who would 'see life,' begin;
It whets the appetite of wealthy sinners
Seeking their *vis-à-vis* for Richmond dinners."

LXXX.

So it was settled. Heaven knows what pact
  Between the pair was furthermore concluded.

One can't say always how one's heroes act,
    And we're quite ignorant of what these two did ;
But there's one positive and patent fact,
    Miss Constance Fitzfulke's name henceforth obtruded
Itself in bills, which said her part would be as
    Julia in the new Bouffe—" Pious Æneas."

LXXXI.

We know the link between them was soon broken,
    That he forgot—and she would not forgive ;—
The usual end of light vows rashly spoken—
    The usual end of *immortelles* we weave
Into a passing fancy's foolish token.
    The Love goes out, and—well, the lovers live,
And, turning o'er some old creased yellow letter,
He cannot, for his life, tell where he met her.

LXXXII.

One lives—with just another cause for saying
    Hard things against the sex which, from our nurses
Unto our widows, lives but for betraying.
    One lives—to vent a few dramatic curses
Upon their heads, and, for our pain's allaying,
    To smoke more pipes, and write more doleful verses,
Such as Jon Duan wrote in the dyspeptic
Tone of the Jilted who would seem a Sceptic.

Vanitas.

I.

Tell me I'm weary ; say of Pride—it cowers ;
    Of love—it bored me ;
    Of faith—love broke it ;
But add, the world's a weed worth all its flowers,
    And fate afford me
    The time to smoke it.

II.

They who pretend that this last joy, disabled
    From pleasing, duly
    Will leave you lonely,
Know not how fortune's wizard-wand has labelled
    The fairy Thule
    " For smokers only ; "

III.

The *dahlias bleus* in courts of Spanish castles,
    And, where it's shady,
    The *merle blanc* chanting,
And floating robes, and feathers, fringe and tassels
    That frame the lady
    One's always wanting.

IV.

How sweet are memories of the thin white bodies,
    When, sooner or later
    Two puffs dismiss them ;
And what love grows for vague lips of the goddess
    When the creator
    Can never kiss them !

V.

Ah, those clouds aid the preachers' exhortations
    With apt examples
    Of hope's fruitions,
And breed, in time, that comfortable patience
    Which mutely tramples
    On vain ambitions.

VI.

The goddess grows amorphous in the fusion
    Of fumes, and none deign
    To mend or drape her—
Hence, stoic smokers draw the trite conclusion
    That most things mundane
    Must end in vapour.

VII.

And in the place of peace, and praise, and laurel,
    A bay-wrecked boat sees,
    From which in deep tone,
Comes o'er the water's waste—the Master's moral
    Of Ματαιότης
    Ματαιοτήτων

LXXXIII.

A first night at the Pandemonium. All
    The *façade* is ablaze. Electric light
Streams from the fronting houses on a wall,
    Bearing in letters, half a yard in height :
" Pious Æneas ; or, the Roman Fall,"—
    With a few witticisms just as bright
(*Vide* the theatre columns of the *Times*),
Filched from the bills of ancient pantomimes.

LXXXIV.

Cabs are *écheloned* in adjoining streets ;
   The first-night clan has mustered in full force :
The critics, who've got pocketfuls of sheets
   Of ready-made abuse or praise, of course ;
Some actors—first nights are their special treats—
   An actress, yearning for that strange divorce
Which hangs fire—not because her lord don't doubt her,
But just because he'd get no parts without her.

LXXXV.

There's the small German banker come to see
   If this thing threatens his majestic place
As millionaire, supporting two or three
   Flourishing houses—not from any base
Desire of pelf, but just to win the key
   Of a few dressing-rooms, to know a brace
Of low comedians—and perhaps arrive at
A knowledge of how authors look in private.

LXXXVI.

There's Rhadamanthus of the *Thunderer*,
   Who generally, to prime himself, dines freely ;
There's Papa Levy, breathing nard and myrrh
   Proffered by Freddy Arnold—styled the Mealy
Gusher—his fond and faithful thurifer,
   There's Sala—with that one jocose and steely
Orb levelled at Hain Friswell like a pistol—
A fierce carbuncle glowing at a crystal.

LXXXVII.

There's bland E. Blanchard, with the sleek curled locks,
   There's the white head that gives the *Athenæum*
Those pure and classic notices ; there flocks
   The Civil Service legion—You should see 'em
Passing pretentiously from box to box,
   Chanting Anathema, or a Te Deum,
According to their hearers' love or spite,
For, or against, the author of the night.

LXXXVIII.

And nameless crowds fill up the stalls ; a hum
   Subdued goes down the critics' own first row ;
Dawdling Guy Livingstones are stricken dumb
   By their profound anxiety to know
Whether Amanda, Lou or Nell will " come
   Out strong "—or make dear friends and rivals crow :
And one by one the detrimentals rise,
And saunter off to see how the ground lies.

LXXXIX.

The secret of this theatre's success
   They know. You pass behind the boxes, thread
Some corridors and galleries that grow less
   Thronged as you push on, save by some well-bred
Patrons profound of drama and the Press :—
   They bribe the latter, by the first are bled ;
You come across a small door where officials
Demand of you your name and *her* initials.

XC.

And you descend a Dantesque staircase, filled
   With that foul feverish air of the *coulisse*,
Into a world where all essay to build,
   Apparently a Babel, not a piece.
At every step you take you're nearly killed
   By carpenters ; by call-boys—cackling geese—
And men who're shifting temples, wings, and drops,
Or handing Grecian goddesses their "props."

XCI.

Only the maëstro is self-possessed
   In this great madhouse, set on fire by night—
That's the comparison that suits it best ;—
   He, humming shreds of opera airs, makes light
Of each defect, because all his hopes rest
   Upon his music, which will set all right ;
Jon Duan, being a novice at the trade,
Though not less vain, was rather more afraid.

XCII.

He gave the worst directions, quite forgetting
   The most important ; he strode to and fro
From prompter to stage manager, upsetting
   The watering pots, with which the dust's laid low,
When all the scene-shifters have finished "setting,"
   He felt a subtle fever stealing thro'
Him—" Author ! " heard, and hisses, madly mingled,
'Twas like champagne drunk through his ears, which tingled.

XCIII.

" Lend me your rouge."—" Miss Amy's borrowed it."
   " The hairdresser ! " — " He's occupied."—
" I'm in

The second scene."—"I'm in the first!"—"A
    chit!"
"A minx!"—"Oh, dresser, take care with
    that pin!"
"Dresser—I'm sure my shoulder-straps will
    split."—
That is the usual last moment's din—
Traversed by call-boy's cries, tenor's objections,
Mechanics' oaths, and author's last directions.

XCIV.

Then Dido came down from her dressing-room.
    Her maid held up her train—she strode
    superb
In sheeny satin—dazzling, with a bloom
    From Rimmel's on that face—that neck you
    curb
But with a diamond necklace. Vague perfume,
    Distilled from many a rare and precious herb,
Enveloped her—as some ethereal presence,
To which all present made profound obeisance.

XCV.

The maëstro bore her poodle, and her fan
    Was carried by the manager. She knew
Her power, the jade! and calmly her gaze ran
    Around the stage. "That chair will never
    do"—
And it was changed. "That drop's too high"—
    a man
Was straightway sent to lower it—they flew,
They bowed, they cringed, and felt it a great
    honour—
Hadn't they spent ten thousand pounds upon her?

XCVI.

Then the bell rings—that tinkle which the
    hearts
Of authors echo with re-tingling force.
The curtain rises, and the public starts
    Quick to its feet, and in a moment's hoarse
With hailing the fair favourite—from all parts
    Bouquets rain down upon her, hurled of course,
By hands that have held her's—and left, too,
    there,
Not a few fortunes poets would call fair.

XCVII.

And the applause ne'er ceased, for no one heard
    A line, but saw legs after legs succeed
Each other, caper and poussette. No word
    Was wanted. All who've come have what they
    need—
Plenty of lime-light, music, and a herd
    Of puppets, pink, and finest of their breed:
That's why the papers next day chronicled
The piece as one in which France was excelled.

XCVIII.

Oh, those encores—those bravoes, how they make
    One's bosom bound, one's vanity brim o'er.
The modest bounds of reticence we break,
    Only behind our inmost chamber's door—
Where, it is true, a rich revenge we take
    For the feigned meekness of an hour before—
But on a first night it's legitimate
To say, as well as feel convinced, you're great.

XCIX.

But o'er Jon Duan's brow a shade would come,
    E'en while Queen Dido ran off, flushed with
    praise,
And said he was "a perfect treasure." Some
    Dim struggling recollections of the plays
He'd hoped to write—ere this indecent dumb
    Show of fine legs—plays, worthy of old days,
And which do one more honour in one's desk,
Perhaps, than many a popular burlesque.

C.

And so, when Dido and Æneas had
    Been called on thrice, he answered to the shout
For "Author! Author!" with a face half sad,
    Half cynical; as, gazing round about,
He saw what philtres made the public mad,
    And why they hissed not those fat women out—
And in his heart he thanked, the while he made
    his
Bow, the dear friends of all his "leading ladies."

Canto The Seventh.

I.

WEARY of London and of London ways,
   The glare and glitter of the London nights,
And very weary also of the days,
   Which once could minister such rare delights,
Duan, who erst had written many lays
   Praising the hundred pleasant sounds and sights
Of this great hive of very busy bees,
Resolved to quit the town and take his ease.

II.

He sometimes liked, although in Fashion's season,
   To bid farewell to sun-dried London streets ;
He could not, nor could we, afford a reason,
   To every stupid questioner one meets
Who pries about, as if suspecting treason,
   To find out why the pulse so languid beats,
Or why we seek the hillside, sea, or river,—
And puts it down to a disordered liver.

III.

So Duan turned to fields and pastures new,
   Taking a ticket for the Midland line;
For on the pleasant shores full well he knew
   He might find scenes to soften and refine ;
And thinking much about the same, he grew
   Almost poetic—till he wished to dine ;
And then he roused from fancy's meditation,
And looked in Bradshaw for the stopping station.

IV.

He crossed the border, and at once he felt
   A keenness and a rawness in the air ;
A fume of oats and cock-a-leekie smelt,
   Heard mingled sounds of blasphemy and prayer ;
And saw that on the people's faces dwelt
   A hard and bony Calvinistic stare,
Which seemed to express it was a Scot's life-labour
To skin a flint and damn outright his neighbour.

V.

O, Caledonia ! very stern and wild,
   And only dear to those who travel through you ;
The poet says you're lov'd by each Scotch child,
   But you do not believe such nonsense, do you?

What Scotchman is there that would not be riled,
  If he was bound for life to stick close to you?
No, Land of heath, and loch, and shaggy moor,
  You're only dear, say we, to those who tour.

VI.

O, Land of Whisky, Oatmeal, Bastards, Bibles;
  O Land of Kirks, Kilts, Claymores, Kail, and
    Cant,—
Of lofty mo .tains and of very high hills,
  Of dreary "Sawbaths," and of patriot rant;
O Land which Dr. Johnson foully libels,
  To sound thy praises does our hero pant;
And to relate how, from engagements freed,
He calmly vegetated north of Tweed.

VII.

He saw "Auld Reekie," climbed up Arthur's Seat,
  And thought the modern Athens a fine city;
Admired the view he got from Prince's Street,
  And wished the lassies could have been more
    pretty—
With sm "er bones, and less decided feet;
  He found the cabmen insolent, though witty;
The Castle "did," and, ere he slept, had been on
The Carlton Hill and seen the new Parthenon.

VIII.

The Edinburg. "Sawbath" bored him, though,
  'Twas like being in a city of the dead;
With solemn steps, and faces full of woe,
  The people to their kirks and chapels sped,
Heard damning doctrines, droned some psalms,
    and so
Went home again with Puritanic tread;
Pulled down their blinds, and in the evening
    glooms,
Got very drunk in t .eir back sitting-rooms.

IX.

All, outward form—it is the old, old story:
  The Pharisee his presence still discloses:—
They go to church, they give to God the glory;
  They roll their eyes, and snuffle through their
    noses;
Tow'rds other sinners hold views sternly gory,
  And are great sticklers for the law of Moses.
Then go home, shut their doors, and, as a body,
Go in for secret sins and too much "toddy."

X.

But westward was the cry, and Duan went
  To Balloch Pier, and steamed up Lomond's
    loch;
And felt inclined for silent sentiment;—
  But tourists crowded round him in a flock,
And vulgarised the scenery, and lent
  A disenchantment to the view; 'tis shock-
ing how they can a fellow-traveller worry,
And bore him with their manners and their
    "Murray."

XI.

They "do" their nature as they would a sum,
  And rule off scenery like so much cash:
They quote their guide-books, or they would be
    dumb:
A waterfall to them is but a splash;
A mountain but so many feet;—they come,
  And go, and see that nature does not clash
With dinner. And take home as travel's fruit
An empty purse and worn-out tourist-suit.

XII.

Soon Duan fled the beaten track, nor rested
  Till, fortunate, he chanced upon a village
From tourist-locusts free, and uninfested
  By Highland landlords who the traveller
    pillage—
A spot with towering mountain-walls invested,
  And given up to pasturage and tillage,
Whilst in the distance, dimly, through a crevice,
You saw the summit of cloud-capp'd Ben Nevis.

XIII.

Here Duan stayed, and fished—there was a burn;
  And flirted—for of course there was a lass
    there;
Tried Gaelic epithets of love to learn;
  Climbed every mountain, and explored each
    pass there,
And set himself, in philosophic turn,
  To study the condition of the mass there;
And found they lived, chiefly on milk and porridge,
In hovels where we wouldn't store up forage.

XIV.

Hovels of mud and peat, with plots of ground
  Just large enough to grow their owner's oats;
A cow, a lank, lean sheep or two he found,
  Some long-legged fowls, and p'rhaps a pair of
    goats:

Inside, nor roofs, nor walls, nor windows sound—
　They're worse than huts of Sclaves, or Czechs,
　　or Croats :
So lives, and will live, till lairds' hearts grow
　softer,
That remnant of the feudal days, the crofter.

XV.

He pays but little rent, but even then
　Body and soul he scarce can keep together :
His wife and daughters have to work like men,
　Subsistence hangs on such a fragile tether ;
And when the snow comes drifting up the glen,
　God knows how they survive the wintry weather.
We fuss about the happy South Sea Islanders,
But have no thought for these half-starving
　Highlanders.

XVI.

He walked through tracts of country—countless
　　acres,—
　White men ejected that red-deer may live ;
And let to rich and purse-proud sugar-bakers,
　Who care not what the rent is that they give ;
Nor that they have been desolation-makers,—
　To use a very mild appelative—
And when he saw these forests so extensive,
Those Highland deer, thought he, were too ex-
　pensive.

XVII.

Sport is a proper thing enough—we are
　No weak and sickly sentimentalists ;
But what *is* sport ? For very, very far
　The definitions differ : one insists
It's battue-shooting ; then, a butcher, bar
　None, is the greatest sportsman that exists—
He's slaughtering always ; not a lord whose study
It is to make big bags, is half as bloody.

XVIII.

A slaughter-house would be a new delight
　For high-born ladies who " warm corners visit,"
And relish pigeon-shooting—'twould excite
　Fresh joys to see a pig stuck, and to quiz it
As it dies slowly with a squeal of fright ;
　For if they like the killing so, why is it
They draw the line at pigeon or at pheasant ?—
To see big beasts killed would be still more
　pleasant.

XIX.

But to our muttons, that is, to our deer—
  Stalking the stag is proper sport, we grant;
But British sport should never interfere
  With British people's welfare—if we can't
Hunt deer unless a country-side's made drear
  And desolate,—why, then it's clear, we shan't
Be acting properly to make a waste
To suit a few rich sportsmen's vulgar taste.

XX.

John Duan heard sad tales of men being turned
  From 'neath their treasured and ancestral roof;
And sheep by thousands could be kept, he learn'd,
  Where now, save for the deer, there roams no hoof;—
He look'd on ruin'd homes, and his heart burned
  With indignation, as he saw fresh proof
Of how the man, with money in his hand,
Can rough-shod ride o'er all the privileged land.*

XXI.

And he came back to England, his heart burning
  To tell his story in the *Daily News*;
Resolved to stay this very general turning
  Of fertile land to desert: but his views
Met with but faint encouragement;—discerning
  Men thought him right: but, just then, to amuse
The public, there came up a new sensation—
Sir Henry Thompson's paper on Cremation.

XXII.

So, up in Scotland there are, still, evictions,
  And still all else gives way to sport and game:
No matter how severe are the inflictions
  On harmless people: still it is the same.
There must be deer and grouse; and soon in fictions
  Alone will live the Highlander's proud name.
Perish the people, and whate'er would war
With rich and selfish pleasures—*Vive le Sport!*

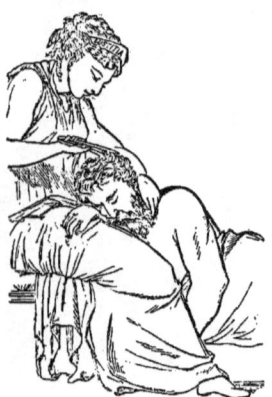

* It is worthy of record that a Scotch nobleman, whose large estate is, by dint of wholesale evictions and purposed neglect, being turned into deer-forests—called forests, seemingly, because they do not contain a single tree—has been able, by the exercise of his lordly will, to prevent the post-office telegraph-wires passing over a part of his property, where, for the convenience of hundreds of isolated people, it would have been especially useful. His lordship's most urgent argument against the wires was that *they would frighten his grouse!* The wires have accordingly made a détour, and his lordship's unfortunate tenants are left practically cut off from the world, to get ill, and get well again, as best they can, and to die without being able to make a sign. Meanwhile, the grouse are not frightened—which is, of course, a great blessing.

Canto The Eighth.

I.

FRAGRANT odour of the choicest weeds,
A hum of voices, pitched in high-born tones ;
A score of fellows, some of our best breeds,
The Heir-apparent to the British throne ;
Soft-footed flunkeys tending to their needs—
The vintage in request, to-night, is Beaune—
Luxurious lounging-chairs, well-stuffed settees,
An air of lavishness, and taste, and ease.

II.

The walls are covered with a set of frames
Containing all the members limned by "Ape";
The loungers bear our most illustrious names,
At which the outside public gasp and gape.
That is a duke's son who just now exclaims—
"Avaunt, ye ' World 'ly and unholy shape ! "
And he who enters, being the " shape " he means,
Is little Labby, fresh from City scenes.

III.

There is more chatter :— " How are 'Anglo's' now ? "—
"Were you at Prince's ?"—"Isn't Amy stunning ? "—
" The bets are off."—",She waltzes like a cow."—
" It's Somerset is making all the running."—
"Churchill's on guard."— "O, yes, a devilish row ! "—
" It's in the *World*."—" I say, Wales, Yorke is punning."—
" The framjous muff ! "—" By Jove ! an awful joke ! "—
Such are the words that penetrate the smoke.

IV.

Guelpho is beaming, as he always beams,
And listening to Jon Duan's latest " tips ";
Upon a sofa Wodecot lies and dreams
Of other hearts, and Nellie's charming lips ;
The air with pretty little scandals teems,
Of men's mistakes and pretty women's slips.
What looked you for within the sacred portals ?—
The Guelpho Clubmen, after all, are mortals.

Again the noiseless door swings open wide,
And Coachington is with a loud roar greeted.

" Is Bromley still by Bow ? " a witling cried,
Before the new arrival could be seated ;
But he—he had sat down by Guelpho's side—
Said, " I bought this outside," and then repeated,
From a broadsheet of ballads, 'midst much laughter,
The " Coster's Carol " you'll find following after.

The Coster's Carol.

1.

I may be rough an' like o' that,
But I ain't no bloomin' fool ;
An' I'm rather up to what is what,
Though I never goed to school.
I know my way about a bit,
An' this is what I say :—
That it's those as does the business
As ought to get the pay !

2.

I ain't no grudge agen the Queen,
Leastways, that is, no spite ;
But I helps to keep her, so I mean
To ax for what's my right :—
An' as she won't come out at all,
It's not no 'arm to say,
That if she don't do the business,
Why, she shouldn't get the pay.

3.

She's livin' on the cheap, I'm told,
An' puttin' lots away—
Some gets like that when they is old—
But what I want's fair play !
Let Wictoria get her pension,
An' up in Scotland stay—
But let them as do her business,
Be the ones to get most pay.

4.

I think as 'ow her eldest son
'As got a hopen 'art ;
I likes his looks, myself, for one,
An' I allus takes his part.
And then there's Alexandrar,
She's a proper sort, I say ;
Them's the two as do the business,
An' they ought to get the pay.

5.

There ain't to me the slightest doubt
　(An' no hoffence I means)—
'Tis the moke as draws the truck about,
　As ought to get most greens.
We do not starve the old 'uns,
　But we give much less to they—
'Tis the ones as do the business
　As ought to have the pay.

6.

I pay my whack for queen or king,
　Like them o' 'igher birth ;
An' 'taint a werry wicked thing
　To want my money's worth :
An' if I'm discontented,
　'Tis only 'cause I say—
That the coves as does the business
　Ought to get the bloomin' pay.

7.

So let the Queen her ways pursoo,
　An' I for one won't weep ;
An' all the idle Jarmints, too,
　As I helps for to keep.
But what I 'ope ain't treason,
　Is boldly for to say
That the Prince and Alexandrar
　Ought to get their mother's pay.

VI.

"What impudence !" they cry, and yet they laugh,
And Duan says, " The logic isn't bad :
A lot of truth is sometimes mixed with chaff.
And, by-the-by, if 't please you, I will add
A parody I've made : on its behalf
I claim your leniency." Then he gave tongue,
And in his rich, ripe voice these verses sung :—

That Germany Jew.

London, 1874.

Which I wish to remark—
　And my language is plain—
That for ways that are dark,
　And tricks far from vain,
The Germany Jew is peculiar,
　Which the same I'm about to explain.

Eim Gott was his name ;
　And I shall not deny
In regard to the same,
　He was wonderful " fly,"
But his watch-chain was vulgar and massive,
　And his manner was dapper and spry.

It's two years come the time,
　Since the mine first came out ;
Which in language sublime
　It was puffed all about :—
But if there's a mine called Miss Emma
　I'm beginning to werry much doubt.

Which there was a small game
　And Eim Gott had a hand
In promoting ! The same
　He did well understand ;
But he sat at Miss Emma's board-table,
　With a smile that was child-like and bland.

Yet the shares they were "bulled,"
　In a way that I grieve,
And the public was fooled,
　Which Eim Gott, I believe,
Sold 22,000 Miss Emmas,
　And the same with intent to deceive.

And the tricks that were played
　By that Germany Jew,
And the pounds that he made
　Are quite well known to you.
But the way that he flooded Miss Emma
　Is a "watering" of shares that is new.

Which it woke up MacD——,
　And his words were but few.
For he said, " Can this be ? "
　And he whistled a " Whew !"
" We are ruined by German-Jew swindlers "!—
　And he went for that Germany Jew.

In the trial that ensued
　I did not take a hand ;
But the Court was quite filled
　With the fi-nancing band,
And Eim Gott was "had" with hard labour,
　For the games he did well understand.

Which is why I remark—
　And my language is plain—
That for ways that are dark,
　And for tricks far from vain.
The Germany Jew was peculiar,—
　But he won't soon be at it again.

VII.

The verdict was "Not bad!" and then the chat
Turned on the Mordaunt Trial and *Vert-Vert*
case :—
"The plaintiff's 'Fairlie' beaten," Jon said ; at
Which witticism there was a grimace ;
Next, little Labby, who till then had sat
Quite quietly, said, at Fred Bates's place
He'd seen a skit, he quite forgot to bring it,
But knew the words, and if they liked, he'd sing it.

"I was with Grant."

"I was with Grant——" the stranger said ;
Said McDougal, "Say no more,
But come you in—I have much to ask—
And please to shut the door."

"I was with Grant——" the stranger said ;
Said McDougal, "Nay, no more,—
You have seen him sit at the Emma board?
Come, draw on your mem'ry's store.

"What said my Albert—my Baron brave,
Of the great financing corps?
I warrant he bore him scurvily
'Midst the interruption's roar!"

"No doubt he did," said the stranger then ;
"But, as I remarked before,
I was with Grant——" "Nay, nay, I know,"
Said McDougal ; "but tell me more.

"He's presented another square!—I see,
You'd smooth the tidings o'er—
Or started, perchance, more Water works
On the Mediterranean shore?

"Or made the Credit Foncier pay,
Or floated a mine with ore?
Oh, tell me not he is pass'd away
From his home in Kensington Gore!"

"I cannot tell," said the unknown man,
"And should have remarked before,
That I was with Grant—Ulysses, I mean—
In the great American war."

Then McDougal spake him never a word,
But beat, with his fist, full sore
The stranger who'd been with Ulysses Grant,
In the great American war. '

VIII.

Then City men they most severely "slated"—
Chiefly the banking German Jew variety.
How is it, Landford asked, cads, aggravated
As they, have wriggled into good society?
And some one said their path to it is plated,
And looked at Guelpho with assumed anxiety.
But Guelpho, ever genial, smiled and said,
"Suppose we have some loo (unlimited)."

IX.

But Duan wouldn't play, but said he'd read
Some of the proofs of his new work instead ;
At which there was a loud outcry, indeed,
And soda corks assailed our hero's head,
Until he promised he would not proceed.
"And, by the way, Jon," Beersford said, "I read
That Lord and Dock's new Annual was out."
Jon shrugged his shoulders, "Yes," he said, "no doubt,

X.

"Very much out indeed ; it seems to me
That Beeton's statement was not far from true,
For from internal evidence I see
He could have had naught with their book to do.
I know him, and whatever he may be,
He is not vulgar ; knows a thing or two ;
Has brains, in fact, and has not got to grovel
In worn-out notions, but goes in for novel."

XI.

And now for loo the cry was raised again,
And there's a general movement towards the door ;
And humming as he went the coster's strain,
Duan, with Guelpho, sought the second-floor.
Said Coming K——, "Come, Duan, please refrain;
Such sentiments, you know, I must deplore."
But Duan—"It's done ; we've put it to the nation—
We've gone in for an Early Abdication!"

END OF JON DUAN.

Spinnings in Town.

I.

Although unversed in lays and ways Byronic,
    And of DON JUAN not a line have read,
Although I've never touched the lyre Ionic,
    And even nursery-rhymes in prose have said,
Yet for a change I'll try the gentle Tonic
    Of verses, that must be with kindness read,
And, being counselled by some good advisers,
Will journey, too—but to see advertisers.

II.

For I have heard a murmur of fair sights,
    All to be seen within gay London town,
Of robes delicious, bonnets gay as sprites,
    Cuirasses braided, and jet-spangled gown.
Inventions useful, such as give delight
    To all good housewives (those that do not frown
At novelty, or, when they're asked to try it,
Say, "It looks very nice, but I shan't buy it.")

III.

Not for such churlish souls, I sing the news—
    Not for the women who don't care for dress;
Our sex's armour ne'er did I refuse,
    And, without *mauvaise honte*, I will confess
That, when I'm asked of two new gowns to choose,
    I do not take the one which costs the less,
Unless 'tis prettier far; and then I say,
" Admire your *sposa's* moderation, pray !"

IV.

I am a SILKWORM, spinner by profession,
    And make long yarns from very slender case,
I love new things and pretty—this confession
    Alone should give me absolution's grace
From all who read my lines and my digression,
    Which I can't really help--words grow apace—
For I could write whole volumes on a feather,
If I had not to put the rhymes together.

V.

Man's dress is of man's life a thing apart:
    To POOLE or MELTON he with calmness goes;
But woman's toilette lies so near her heart,
    That 'tis with doubts, and fears, and many throes

In visiting the rounds of shop and mart,
   That she selects a ribbon or a rose.
Her fate in life doth oft depend, I ween,
   If she be struck with *just that* shade of green.

VI.

Beauteous Hibernia! (Britons, do not frown
   At rhapsodies from one who owes her much)
What could one do without a poplin gown,
   Whose folds take graceful form from every touch?
These lips have never pressed the Blarney "stone"—
   No flattery 'tis to speak of fabrics such
As are produced in Inglis-Tinckler factory—
   Oh dear me! all these rhymes are so refractory.

VII.

To Ireland, too, we owe a great invention;
   For warmth and comfort in the wintry cold,
The ULSTER COAT is just the thing to mention,
   For driving to the covert, or be rolled
In, for the morning train, or GREAT EXTENSION
   LINE TERMINUS, within its cosy fold,
Nor snow nor wet shall harm you, if but ye
Buy ULSTER COATS alone of JOHN MCGEE.

VIII.

Say what you will about furs in cold weather,
   Sing of the warmth of seal skin as you please,
'Gainst cold, or ice, or snow, or all together,
   Give me the ULSTER OVERCOAT of frieze!
Useful in Autumn, driving the heather;
   Safeguard in Winter against cough or sneeze;
But, as they imitate the ULSTER COAT,
See that the maker's name (MCGEE) you note.*

IX.

LADIES' COSTUMES, and SUITS of IRISH stuff,
   WINDERMERE lining, soft, of every shade,
Cuirasses *matelassé* see enough
   To turn the head of either wife or maid.
I think no woman born could ever "huff"
   If in such lovely garments but arrayed,
So, Fathers, Husbands, Brothers, try to find
If "LADIES' ULSTER COATS" won't suit your womankind.

* John G. McGee and Co., Belfast, Ireland.

X.

And for yourselves, who to the coverts go,
   In dog-cart neat, oft in the pouring rain,
The ULSTER DEER-STALKER'S a coat that so
   Will keep you dry, and save rheumatic pain.
It useful is in travelling, to and fro
   The country station, and must prove a gain.
'Tis so becoming to a figure tall!
In fact, it suits all mankind, great and small.

XI.

Where to begin, and whither wend my way!
   Shall I to ATKINSON or JAY first go?
Look at BLACK SILK COSTUMES sold cheap by JAY;
   Or view chairs, tables, carpets, row by row;
Inspect the "Brussels, five-and-two," or say,
   "Prices of furniture I wish to know;"
Look at the mirrors, view the marquet'rie,
Gaze at the inlaid work, or wander free?

XII.

Through gall'ries large, and through saloons light, vast,
   I cast a hasty glance on either hand,
Rich CARVINGS chaste, CRETONNES so bright, and fast
   Colours. I note enough to deck the land
With CURTAINS, COVERS, that will surely last
   When Time has ta'en the pencil from this hand,
Which strives to give a notion (somewhat faint)
Of furniture that would tempt e'en a saint.

XIII.

Talk of Temptation! just call in at JAY'S!
   The LONDON MOURNING WAREHOUSES, I mean,
In Regent Street; 'tis crowded on fine days
   With the *élite* of London, and the Queen
Has patronised the house, and without *lèse-Majesté*, I may mention she has seen
Such crêpe of English and of foreign make,
That from no other house she will it take.

XIV.

Yet at the present moment 'tis not crêpe,
   But SILK COSTUMES that I would bid all see
(SIX POUNDS SIXTEEN!) of the last cut and shape
   The best Parisian MODELS! flowing free,

The graceful folds from dainty bows escape,
  Harmonious corsages with the skirts agree;
See what a change French politics have made—
Silks cost just double when they Nap. obeyed!

XV.

Then there's another JAY, whose house full well
  Both English maids and New York matrons know;
"The best store out for *lingerie, du* tell,"
'Tis near unto the mourning warehouse, so
You can't mistake the *maison* SAMUEL
  JAY, of high renown for brides' trousseaux,
Infants' layettes, and morning toilettes cozy
(For my part, I like cashmere, blue or rosy).

XVI.

Those who do mourn, or wish to compliment
  Acquaintances, connections, or their friends,
Who do not care to see much money spent
  (For crape turns brown, and ravels at the ends),
Should get the ALBERT CRAPE, an EXCELLENT
  CRAPE, good to look at; it intends
To be the only crape used; GOOD and CHEAP—
  Considerations strong for those who weep.

XVII.

Being close by, what hinders me to visit
  The WANZER COMPANY, GREAT PORTLAND STREET?—
The LITTLE WANZER, a machine exquisite—
  With such a lockstitch, sewing is a treat;
It works away on any stuff, nor is it
  One of those kind whose stitching is not neat;
Though small, it sews as well as WANZER D,
  Or WANZER F—"machine for family."

XVIII.

Why trouble we to stitch by midnight taper,
  New cuffs and collars for our future wear,
When we can buy our LINGERIE of PAPER,
  Each day put on a parure, white and fair?
COLLARS, which keep their stiffness 'spite of vapour,
  CUFFS fit for maid and matron *debonair*.
COLLARS and CUFFS, shirt-fronts for gentleman—
  These are in Holborn sold, by EDWARD TANN.

XIX.

Holborn the High, number three hundred eight,
  There one can buy all kinds of paper things,—
Japanese curtains, and *jupons* for state
  Occasions, 'broidered all in wheels and rings.
The paper well doth 'broidery simulate,
  'Tis raised and open; then the're blinds and strings,
Of paper all, most curious to view—
  Think of the saving in the washing, too!

XX.

How difficult it is to find out rhymes
  For VOSE'S PORTABLE ANNIHILATOR,
Which gardens waters, fires checks betimes!
  Or LOYSEL'S HYDROSTATIC PERCOLATOR
For making coffee in,—oh Christmas chimes!
  I can't find any rhyme except Equator,
And that means naught: I want the world to know it,
  They're made at BIRMINGHAM by GRIFFITHS, BROWETT.

XXI.

Respite is near, or surely I'd be undone;
  'Tis one o'clock, and time to have some lunch.
Where shall I turn? Of course unto the LONDON,
  Where, in the Ladies' Room, we find *Fun*, *Punch*,
To while the time we spend on things so mundane
  (As well as other papers), while we munch
Good things, and *menus* gay and *cartes* unravel,
  Learn that the restaurant is kept by REED and CAVELL.

XXII.

THE LONDON RESTAURANT is famed for DINNERS,
  (The London is in Fleet Street, by the way,
Close unto Temple Bar); too good for sinners,
  By far the dinner that is set each day.
I took my lads there when not out of "pinners,"
  The first time that they ever saw a play.
When children go to see the Pantomime,
  'Tis at THE LONDON they should stop and dine.

XXIII.

The SKATING SUITS for ladies next claim my
  Attention, for the weather's very cold;

These suits are useful both for wet and dry
    Weather, and drapèd are in graceful fold,
Shorter or longer, looped up low or high,
    Forming jupons by means of ribbons' hold ;—
And these costumes, accompanied by muff
To match, and edged with fur, are warm enough

XXIV.

To keep each *jolie frileuse* free from harm,
    E'en in Siberia's frozen climate drear ;
Where everlasting snows keep endless calm,
    And toes are nipped up in a way that here
We cannot comprehend, nor guess what charm
    Keeps men alive, far from all they hold dear—
I'm sure that I should die could I not meet
A friend and go to shop in Conduit Street.

XXV.

Where, by the bye, ladies will always find,
    At BENJAMIN'S, cloth habits to their taste ;
And will discover, if they have a mind,
    Most useful pleated skirts, in which a waist
(That's pretty in itself) looks most refined,
    And tapers from the folds, if neatly laced.
Dear dames, if you will give my words fair weight,
Call in Conduit Street at NUMBER THIRTY-EIGHT.

XXVI.

But if indeed, you will "TAKE MY ADVICE,"
    As well as all "THINGS that YOU OUGHT to KNOW,"
You'll go for DIARIES and books so nice
    Unto JAMES BLACKWOOD'S, PATERNOSTER ROW,
Where information's given in a trice,
    On Pocket Books and Diaries, and so
Cheap are these works that there is no excuse
Left, if these diaries you do not use.

XXVII.

But wherefore ask for clever Cooking Book,
    If open fires are seen where'er one roves,
Or why on coloured illustrations lock,
    If that we can't have SOLAR cooking Stoves;
Oh ! joyful news for housewives and for cooks !—
    PORTABLE, too, fancy a stove that moves
Easily ! Yet these stoves are to be seen
At Bishopsgate Street Within, at BROWN and
    GREEN.

XXVIII.

Auriferous visions on my eyeballs strike—
    No imitation, it *must* be real gold,
This jewell'ry made by the Brothers PYKE ;
    Yet 'tis but ABYSSINIAN, we are told ;
How difficult to credit ! It's so like
    To eighteen carat that we're often "sold."
As for pickpockets, I have heard that they
Have left off stealing chains, finding they may

XXIX.

No profit get from GOLD that is AS GOOD
    As the real, veritable Simon Pure ;
So, honest turn these rogues, once understood
    Among their set, that profits come no more.—
With ABYSSINIAN gold to clasp one's hood,
    We safely stand at Covent Garden's door ;
For many a thief has got in sad disgrace
For gold made by THE PYKES in ELY PLACE.

XXX.

To wear with Abyssinian Golden chain,
    A cheap and good watch you will get of DYER,
At NUMBER NINETY, REGENT STREET; remain
    Till you have seen the watches you require,
SUPERIOR LEVERS, PATENT KEYLESS—gain,
    These watches don't, or lose ; at prices higher
You may have watches, but not better see
Than *Dyer's* WATCHES, CLOCKS, and JEWELLERY.

XXXI.

Oh, for the pen of Byron, or such a wight
    Who could help a poor rhymster in a fix !
How can I e'er explain that MR. HIGHT
    's invented a REVOLVING CIPHER DISC.
Easy to execute by day or night,
    Yet difficult to solve or to unmix
The cipher, and from all suspicion clear ;
Essentials held by BACON and NAPIER.

XXXII.

To rest awhile from "ciphering" my brain,
    I turn to PICTURES of fair SCENERY—
THE UPPER ALPINE WORLD—again, again,
    These visions fair by LOPPE I would see :
They're shown in Conduit Street ; and I would fain
    Return unto that lovely gallery—
Pictures by LOPPE please me so, I'm willing
For six days in the week to pay my shilling.

XXXIII.

A shilling is a pretty little sum,
   And with three halfpence added, we can get
Almost each PILL that's made ; let's count them ; come
   And see if the long list I do know yet—
I ought to, for the press is never dumb
   Upon the merits of the whole, round set ;
Thinking with THACKERAY, that we shall find
A favourite pill with each " well-ordered mind."

XXXIV.

First, GRAINS OF HEALTH must stand, because they're new
   And TASTELESS, being COATED o'er with PEARL,
I think they're DR. RIDGE'S ; 'tis he who
   Gives us digestive biscuits fit for girl,
Or infant delicate ; truth, there are few
   Dyspeptics who don't take them. Where's the churl
Who will not try, to ease life's many ills,
A single remedy, say ROBERTS' PILLS.

XXXV.

PAGE WOODCOCK, too, has made a wondrous name
   For curing every ill that you may mention ;
While BRODIE'S cures (MIRACULOUS) the same
   For CORNS and BUNIONS :—it was my intention
To name CLARKE'S BLOOD MIXTURE, of which the fame
   Is well established ; but I must my pen shun,
If I go on like this : I really feel
My hair turns grey while rhyming—where's LA-TREILLE?

XXXVI.

RESTORING and PRODUCING all one's hair
   Within short time and on the baldest place :
" Waiting for copy !" is the cry, so there,
   I cannot mention half I would, with grace :—
WRIGHT'S PILOSAGINE, EADE'S PILLS for pain in face—
And yet I think 'twould really be a scandal
If I omit the HAIR RESTORER : SANDELL.

XXXVII.

For New Year's Offering, and for Christmas Box,
   ROWLAND'S ODONTO, and MACASSAR OIL,
With ROWLANDS' KALYDOR, which really mocks
   Youth's bloom, removing trace of time and toil.
For JEWEL-SAFES and THIEF-DETECTING LOCKS
   Try CHUBB, his patent safes will always foil
Both fire and thief, do with them all they can—
A first-rate present for a gentleman !

XXXVIII.

While for the ladies, surely you can't err,
   To buy for them a WHIGHT and MANN MA-CHINE,
For hand or foot, indeed this will please her,
   Whom you denominate your household Queen :
But as some women dearly love to stir
   Abroad to choose their presents, then I ween,
You will do well to take her some morn,
To buy a new machine in famed Holborn.

XXXIX.

In CHARLES STREET, NUMBER FOUR, you'll find that SMITH
   And CO. have of MACHINES a various stock ;
There you can test machines and see the pith
   Of all their varied workings—chain and lock.
Oh, for the pen of Owen Meredith,
   That I no more with such bad rhymes need shock
Your feelings ; but, remember, while you're there,
To look at WEIR'S MACHINES, also in SOHO SQUARE.

XL.

Taking one's teeth out is a painful thing ;—
   We don't much like this parting with our bones ;—
But what if PAINLESS DENTISTRY I sing,
   Which all mankind can have from MR. JONES ?
Of all the new inventions 'tis the king.
   Imagine teeth out, minus all the groans !
We'll turn to other subjects, if you please,
A GUINEA BUNCH of TWENTY-FIVE ROSE TREES.

XLI.

This is a Christmas-box for those who love
   Their gardens ; and GEORGE COOLING'S nursery, BATH,
Roses supplies in quantities above
   This number at a cheaper rate : he hath

Collections good, as many prizes prove,
Taken for roses for the bed or path.
Another swift transition if you please,
Go to H. WEBBER for your CHRISTMAS CHEESE.

XLII.

With cheese we want good wine; and, as the short
Old-fashioned phrase is, "Good wine needs no
bush,"
So I name simply HEDGES-BUTLER'S PORT,
Sure that when you your chair backward do push
The vintage will not upon you retort
With sudden seizure or with gouty rush.
In fact, I'm told you may drink many pledges
In wine that's bought of BUTLER and of HEDGES.

XLIII.

How can I possibly find rhymes to fit
The MAGNETICON, or SYCHNOPHYLAX;
Even our well-beloved OZOKERIT
Candles, which do so much resemble wax,
Not easy are to verse on; I will quit
These subjects, and try if OPOPONAX,
Sweetest of perfumes, will not yield me any.
Oh, yes! here's one—PIESSE'S FRANGIPANNI.

XLIV.

PIESSE and LUBIN an oasis make,
All in the foggy air of New Bond Street;
At number two, their resting place they take,
Filling surroundings with their odours sweet.
LION ALOES, Turkish pastiles for your sake,
Oh, English maids, to make your charms complete.
Ladies, indeed, you will have cause to bless
The labours skilled of LUBIN and PIESSE.

XLV.

No space is left of BRAGG'S CARBON to speak,
Or mention STEVENSON'S new FIREWOOD;
To praise SLACK'S SPOONS and FORKS would take
a week,
Or CROSBY'S ELIXIR for cough so good;
MAGNETINE (D'ARLOW'S patent for the weak),
Or BARNARD'S pretty NOVELTIES in WOOD;
The "EASTERN CONDIMENT" for our cold mutton,
And GREEN and CADBURY'S THE VERY BUTTON.

XLVI.

MOSES and SON require an annual quite
Unto themselves to simply name their stock;
OETZMANN'S CARPETS all the world delight,
And scraps for SCREENS are sold by James Lock
CHOCOLAT MENIER is the thing for night
And morning meals. You can physicians mock
If you but take—indeed I am not *maline*—
A daily draught of the PYRETIC SALINE.

XLVII.

Who can explain why Stoneham, of Cheapside,
Should of EACH SHILLING SPENT, THREEPENCE
RETURN
Unto the buyer? and in fact has tried,
By this means, custom to his till to turn;
Succeeded, too : hath not the public hied
To him, and "come" like butter in a churn.
Pour moi, I feel so very, very cross,
When in a crowd, that THREEPENCE GAINED is
loss.

XLVIII.

FLEET'S MINERAL WATERS next demand a word;
DIETZ and CO. have lamps not to be slighted—
Where these burn grumbling tones are never
heard—
The largest room by PARAGON'S well lighted.
There are so many, that 'tis quite absurd,
With ASSER-SHERWIN'S bags I am delighted;
Their WEDDING PRESENTS and their WRITING
CASES
Will bring a blush of joy to merry faces.

XLIX.

In dear old Shakespeare I have often read
Of "bourne from which no traveller returns,"
And an idea will come into my head,
Just think of *never leaving* ADDLEY BOURNE'S,
Renowned for TROUSSEAUX and for CRADLE-BEDS,
INFANTS' LAYETTES—fair *robes de chambre*—one
learns
Such trimmings, sees such treasures—willy, nilly,
We can't keep long away from PICCADILLY.

L.

A change comes o'er the spirit of my dream,
 Where I have often stood I seem to stand,
Sweet odours on my aching senses stream—
 I'm opposite to RIMMEL in the STRAND,
Whose kindly influence on our homes doth beam,
 And fills with joy each child's heart in the land,
Where we behold his CHRISTMAS NOVELTIES,
His PERFUMED ALMANACS, and such things as
 these:

LI.

The robin, and the toys for CHRISTMAS TREES,
 The COMIC ALMANAC and FAN BOUQUET,
Delicious scents and perfumes that do seize
 Upon the weary brain:—restore the gay
And cheerful tone, and give the headache ease.
 All these we owe to him, who holdeth sway
O'er all sweet scents! Ye perfumed sachets tell
 This great magician's name! It is—it is—RIMMEL!

LII.

And now my pen from weary hand doth fall,
 And with humility I lay aside
A task which p'raps some spinners might appal;
 But pleasant has it been to me to glide
From one to other subject, touching all
 With kindly hand, and what doth me betide
At critic's pen I care not, for the rest
I've done, *comme toujours*, just my "level best."

THE SILKWORM.

MYRA, late Editress of BEETONS "YOUNG ENGLISHWOMAN."

MYRA'S JOURNAL of DRESS & FASHION.

In Illustrated Wrapper.

Containing Sixteen Pages, Large Quarto, size of the London Journal, Bow Bells, &c.

PRICE TWOPENCE, MONTHLY.

I PROPOSE to issue, every month, beginning next February, a Journal for Ladies, which shall contain Instructions and Advice in connection with Dress and Fashion.

Several different departments will be necessary to make this Journal useful to the thousands of Ladies whom I hope to have as Subscribers or Correspondents.

Original Articles from Paris, contributed by Madame GOUBAUD, will appear, from which a knowledge will be gained of the newest Materials and coming Modes.

Mademoiselle AGNES VERBOOM, long a Contributor to Mr. BEETON'S Fashion Journals here, and to the leading Lady's Paper in America, will write a Monthly Letter on the Changes in Fashion.

Diagrams, full-sized, for cutting out all kinds of Articles of Dress, will be issued every month; and frequently Paper Models themselves will be issued with MYRA'S JOURNAL.

From the Grand Magasin du Louvre, the first house in Paris, I shall receive bulletins of their latest Purchases, and accounts of what is most in vogue in the Capital of Fashion.

For my personal writing, I shall continue the same plan which I originated, under the name of MYRA, in Mr. BEETON'S "YOUNG ENGLISHWOMAN." Mr. BEETON no longer edits that Journal, and MYRA'S Letters will not appear there in future.

My Letters there were so successful, and the Advice I was able to give seemed so prized by my Correspondents, that I believe I shall be doing some service by devoting the whole space of a Monthly Journal to the subjects of TASTE AND ECONOMY in Dress, and the Alteration of Dress.

I shall, therefore, every month, answer all Correspondents who seek information upon

WHAT DRESSES TO WEAR
AND
HOW TO ALTER DRESSES.

I will pay the most careful attention to any Letters sent me, so that I may answer enquiries with the closest and most exact details; and whilst giving Instructions as to the best Style of Dress and the Alteration of Dress, I shall be anxious to state what is *not* to be done, as well as what *is* to be done, in the important matter of the Toilette.

Letters from Correspondents received by me not later than the 20th of the month will be answered in the next MYRA'S JOURNAL. But all enquiries should be made of me, as much as possible, at the beginning of the month, so as to give me ample time to obtain and prepare particular information on any knotty point.

A Free Exchange, gratis, and open to all who have Articles to dispose of, or barter for others, will be opened in MYRA'S JOURNAL. The Addresses of Exchangers must be printed, in order to have the benefit of the Free Exchange. Addresses, however, can be entered upon the payment of One Shilling in postage stamps, to defray necessary expenses. Rules in connection with the Exchange will be found in MYRA'S JOURNAL.

Some Ladies, on certain occasions, are anxious to receive immediately information as to what is the proper kind of Dress to Wear, or how to Alter the Dresses that they have. To serve these Ladies, I will state in writing, by return of post, what is the best course for them to take. When questions are thus asked for, to be answered by post, enquiries must be accompanied by twelve postage stamps, for expenses of various kinds which will naturally be incurred

---

All Communications to be addressed to MYRA, *care of* WELDON & CO., 15, *Wine Office Court, London, E.C.*

J. OGDEN AND CO., PRINTERS, 172, ST. JOHN STREET, LONDON, E.C.

www.ingramcontent.com/pod-product-compliance
Lightning Source LLC
Chambersburg PA
CBHW031411160426
43196CB00007B/971